CONFIGURING PROCUREMENT AND SOURCING WITHIN DYNAMICS 365 FOR FINANCE & OPERATIONS

MODULE 2: **CONFIGURING PROCUREMENT CATEGORIES**

MURRAY FIFE

ISBN-13: 978-1078195829

Preface

What You Need for this Guide

All the examples shown in this blueprint were done with the Microsoft Dynamics 365 for Operations hosted image that was provisioned through Lifecycle Services.

The following list of software from the virtual image was leveraged within this guide:

Microsoft Dynamics 365 for Operations

Even though all the preceding software was used during the development and testing of the recipes in this book, they should also work on later versions without any changes.

Errata

Although we have taken every care to ensure the accuracy of our content, mistakes do happen. If you find a mistake in one of our books—may be a mistake in the text or the code—we would be grateful if you would report this to us. By doing so, you can save other readers from frustration and help us improve subsequent versions of this book. If you find any errata, please report them by emailing editor@dynamicscompanions.com.

Piracy

Piracy of copyright material on the Internet is an ongoing problem across all media. If you come across any illegal copies of our works, in any form, on the Internet, please provide us with the location address or website name immediately so that we can pursue a remedy.

Please contact us at legal@dynamicscompanions.com with a link to the suspected pirated material.

We appreciate your help in protecting our authors and our ability to bring you valuable content.

Questions

You can contact us at help@dynamicscompanions.com if you are having a problem with any aspect of the book, and we will do our best to address it.

Table of Contents

DYNAMICS COMPANIONS
BARE BONES CONFIGURATION GUIDE

CONFIGURING PROCUREMENT AND SOURCING WITHIN DYNAMICS 365 FOR FINANCE & OPERATIONS
MODULE 2: CONFIGURING PROCUREMENT CATEGORIES

CONFIGURING PROCUREMENT CATEGORIES

Sometimes spending a little bit of time in advance can save you a lot of time in the long run. One example of this is that if you set up the **Procurement Categories** within Procurement and Sourcing, you will be able to use them later on in setup time. So in this chapter we will show you how you can set them up and link them with you Products and Vendors.

Topics Covered

- Configuring Procurement Hierarchies

- Review

www.dynamicscompanions.com
Dynamics Companions

- 7 -

www.blindsquirrelpublishing.com
© 2019 Blind Squirrel Publishing, LLC , All Rights Reserved

BLIND SQUIRREL
PUBLISHING

DYNAMICS COMPANIONS
BARE BONES CONFIGURATION GUIDE

CONFIGURING PROCUREMENT AND SOURCING WITHIN DYNAMICS 365 FOR FINANCE & OPERATIONS
MODULE 2: CONFIGURING PROCUREMENT CATEGORIES

Configuring Procurement Hierarchies

The **Procurement Categories** are all based of a category hierarchy that you set up within Dynamics 365. So the first step is to build a **Category Hierarchy** that you will then link to the Procurement & Sourcing module.

Topics Covered

- Opening up the Category Hierarchies maintenance form

- Creating a new Procurement Category Hierarchy

- Creating a Top Level Procurement Category Node

- Configuring Category Hierarchy Types

- Assigning Products To Procurement Categories

- Assigning Vendors To Procurement Categories

- Inheriting Approved Vendors From Parent Categories

DYNAMICS COMPANIONS
BARE BONES CONFIGURATION GUIDE

CONFIGURING PROCUREMENT AND SOURCING WITHIN DYNAMICS 365 FOR FINANCE & OPERATIONS
MODULE 2: CONFIGURING PROCUREMENT CATEGORIES

Opening up the Category Hierarchies maintenance form

To start off we will want to open up the **Category Hierarchies** maintenance form that we will use to configure all of our procurement categories within the system.

How to do it...

Step 1: Open the Category hierarchies form through the menu

We can get to the **Category hierarchies** form a couple of different ways. The first way is through the master menu.

Navigate to Procurement and sourcing > Setup > Categories and attributes > Category hierarchies.

Step 2: Open the Catagory hierarchies form through the menu search

Another way that we can find the **Catagory hierarchies** form is through the menu search feature.

Type in **catagory h** into the menu search and select **Catagory hierarchies**.

www.dynamicscompanions.com
Dynamics Companions

- 9 -

www.blindsquirrelpublishing.com
© 2019 Blind Squirrel Publishing, LLC, All Rights Reserved

BLIND SQUIRREL
PUBLISHING

DYNAMICS COMPANIONS
BARE BONES CONFIGURATION GUIDE

CONFIGURING PROCUREMENT AND SOURCING WITHIN DYNAMICS 365 FOR FINANCE & OPERATIONS
MODULE 2: CONFIGURING PROCUREMENT CATEGORIES

Opening up the Category Hierarchies maintenance form

How to do it...

Step 1: Open the Category hierarchies form through the menu

We can get to the **Category hierarchies** form a couple of different ways. The first way is through the master menu.

To do this, open up the navigation panel, expand out the **Modules** and group, and click on **Procurement and sourcing** to see all of the menu items that are available. Then click on the **Category hierarchies** menu item within the **Categories and attributes** folder of the **Setup** group.

www.dynamicscompanions.com
Dynamics Companions

- 10 -

www.blindsquirrelpublishing.com
© 2019 Blind Squirrel Publishing, LLC , All Rights Reserved

BLIND SQUIRREL
PUBLISHING

DYNAMICS COMPANIONS
BARE BONES CONFIGURATION GUIDE

CONFIGURING PROCUREMENT AND SOURCING WITHIN DYNAMICS 365 FOR FINANCE & OPERATIONS
MODULE 2: CONFIGURING PROCUREMENT CATEGORIES

Opening up the Category Hierarchies maintenance form

How to do it...

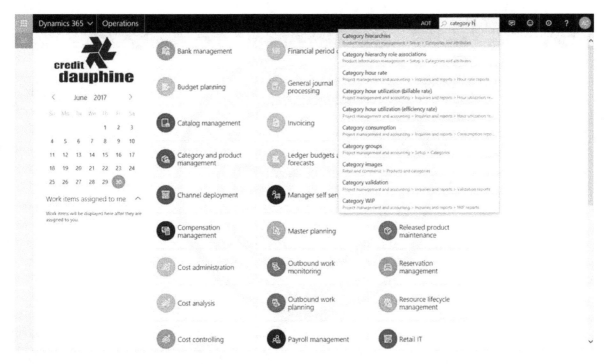

Step 2: Open the Catagory hierarchies form through the menu search

Another way that we can find the **Catagory hierarchies** form is through the menu search feature.

We can do this by clicking on the search icon in the header of the form (or by pressing **ALT+G**) and then type in **catagory h** storage into the search box. Then you will be able to select the **Catagory hierarchies** form from the dropdown list.

dync
www.dynamicscompanions.com
Dynamics Companions

- 11 -

www.blindsquirrelpublishing.com
© 2019 Blind Squirrel Publishing, LLC , All Rights Reserved

BLIND SQUIRREL
PUBLISHING

DYNAMICS COMPANIONS
BARE BONES CONFIGURATION GUIDE

CONFIGURING PROCUREMENT AND SOURCING WITHIN DYNAMICS 365 FOR FINANCE & OPERATIONS
MODULE 2: CONFIGURING PROCUREMENT CATEGORIES

Opening up the Category Hierarchies maintenance form

How to do it...

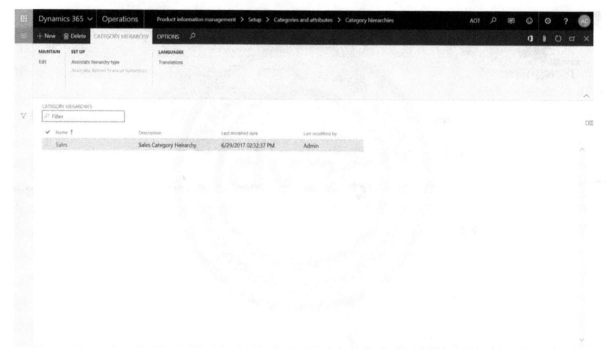

Step 2: Open the Catagory hierarchies form through the menu search

This will open up the **Category hierarchies** maintenance form where we will be able to see all of the different categories that we have already set up.

www.dynamicscompanions.com
Dynamics Companions

- 12 -

www.blindsquirrelpublishing.com
© 2019 Blind Squirrel Publishing, LLC , All Rights Reserved

BLIND SQUIRREL
PUBLISHING

DYNAMICS COMPANIONS
BARE BONES CONFIGURATION GUIDE

CONFIGURING PROCUREMENT AND SOURCING WITHIN DYNAMICS 365 FOR FINANCE & OPERATIONS
MODULE 2: CONFIGURING PROCUREMENT CATEGORIES

Creating a new Procurement Category Hierarchy

Right now there is only one category hierarchy defined in the system, and that is for the Sales area. We will want to create a new category hierarchy that we can use just for the procurement area within the system.

How to do it...

Step 1: Click New

We will start this process off by adding a new category hierarchy.

Click on the **New** button.

Step 2: Update the Name

Now we will give our new category hierarchy a name to reference it by.

Set the Name to Procurement.

Step 3: Update the Description

And then we will want to give our hierarchy a more detailed description.

Set the Description to Procurment Category Hierarchy.

www.blindsquirrelpublishing.com
© 2019 Blind Squirrel Publishing, LLC , All Rights Reserved

BLIND SQUIRREL
PUBLISHING

DYNAMICS COMPANIONS
BARE BONES CONFIGURATION GUIDE

CONFIGURING PROCUREMENT AND SOURCING WITHIN DYNAMICS 365 FOR FINANCE & OPERATIONS
MODULE 2: CONFIGURING PROCUREMENT CATEGORIES

Creating a new Procurement Category Hierarchy

How to do it...

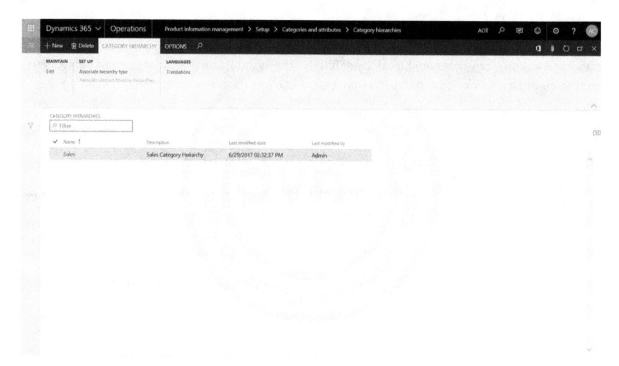

Step 1: Click New

We will start this process off by adding a new category hierarchy.

To do this just click on the **New** button.

dync
www.dynamicscompanions.com
Dynamics Companions

- 14 -

www.blindsquirrelpublishing.com
© 2019 Blind Squirrel Publishing, LLC, All Rights Reserved

BLIND SQUIRREL
PUBLISHING

DYNAMICS COMPANIONS
BARE BONES CONFIGURATION GUIDE

CONFIGURING PROCUREMENT AND SOURCING WITHIN DYNAMICS 365 FOR FINANCE & OPERATIONS
MODULE 2: CONFIGURING PROCUREMENT CATEGORIES

Creating a new Procurement Category Hierarchy

How to do it...

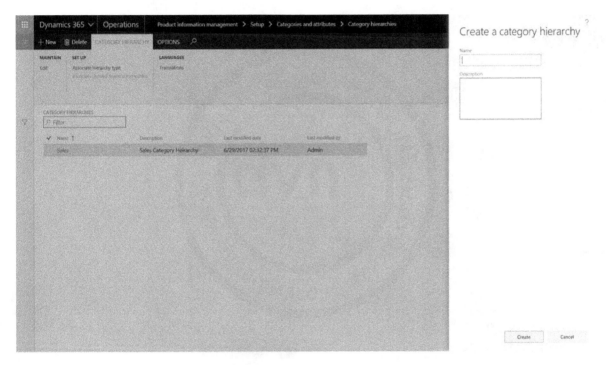

Step 1: Click New

This will open up a new dialog panel that will allow us to start defining our procurement category hierarchy.

www.dynamicscompanions.com
Dynamics Companions

- 15 -

www.blindsquirrelpublishing.com
© 2019 Blind Squirrel Publishing, LLC , All Rights Reserved

BLIND SQUIRREL
PUBLISHING

DYNAMICS COMPANIONS
BARE BONES CONFIGURATION GUIDE

CONFIGURING PROCUREMENT AND SOURCING WITHIN DYNAMICS 365 FOR FINANCE & OPERATIONS
MODULE 2: CONFIGURING PROCUREMENT CATEGORIES

Creating a new Procurement Category Hierarchy

How to do it...

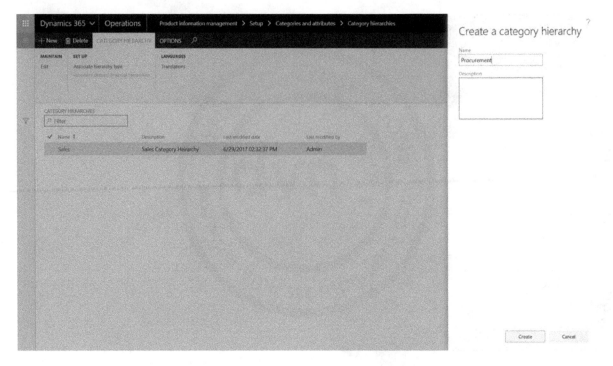

Step 2: Update the Name

Now we will give our new category hierarchy a name to reference it by.

To do this we will just need to update the **Name** value.

For this example, we will want to set the **Name** to **Procurement**.

dync
www.dynamicscompanions.com
Dynamics Companions

- 16 -

www.blindsquirrelpublishing.com
© 2019 Blind Squirrel Publishing, LLC , All Rights Reserved

BLIND SQUIRREL
PUBLISHING

DYNAMICS COMPANIONS
BARE BONES CONFIGURATION GUIDE

CONFIGURING PROCUREMENT AND SOURCING WITHIN DYNAMICS 365 FOR FINANCE & OPERATIONS
MODULE 2: CONFIGURING PROCUREMENT CATEGORIES

Creating a new Procurement Category Hierarchy

How to do it...

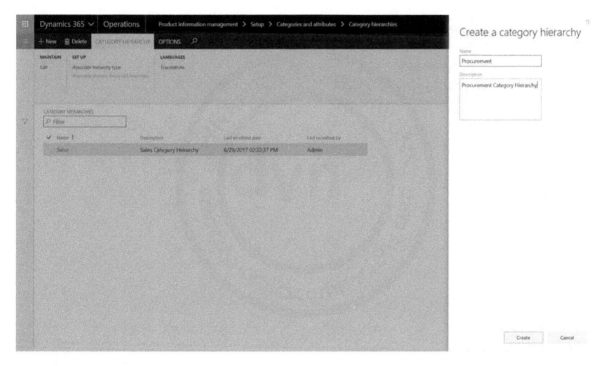

Step 3: Update the Description

And then we will want to give our hierarchy a more detailed description.

To do this we will just need to update the **Description** value.

For this example, we will want to set the **Description** to **Procurment Category Hierarchy**.

www.dynamicscompanions.com
Dynamics Companions

- 17 -

www.blindsquirrelpublishing.com
© 2019 Blind Squirrel Publishing, LLC , All Rights Reserved

BLIND SQUIRREL
PUBLISHING

DYNAMICS COMPANIONS
BARE BONES CONFIGURATION GUIDE

CONFIGURING PROCUREMENT AND SOURCING WITHIN DYNAMICS 365 FOR FINANCE & OPERATIONS
MODULE 2: CONFIGURING PROCUREMENT CATEGORIES

Creating a new Procurement Category Hierarchy

How to do it...

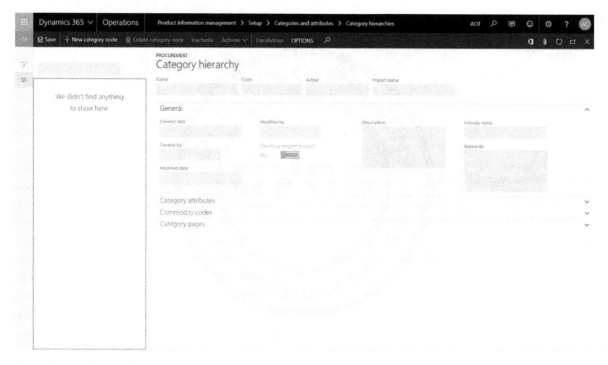

Step 3: Update the Description

This will take us to a new form where we will be able to start building our Procurement Category Hierarchy.

dync
www.dynamicscompanions.com
Dynamics Companions

- 18 -

www.blindsquirrelpublishing.com
© 2019 Blind Squirrel Publishing, LLC , All Rights Reserved

BLIND SQUIRREL
PUBLISHING

DYNAMICS COMPANIONS
BARE BONES CONFIGURATION GUIDE

CONFIGURING PROCUREMENT AND SOURCING WITHIN DYNAMICS 365 FOR FINANCE & OPERATIONS
MODULE 2: CONFIGURING PROCUREMENT CATEGORIES

Creating a Top Level Procurement Category Node

Now we will want to set up the top most level of the Procurement Category Hierarchy that we will attach all of our main procurement categories to.

How to do it...

Step 1: Click New

At this point we will want to add our first Category Hierarchy node.

Click on the **New** button.

Step 2: Update the Name

Now we will want to rename the Category hierarchy

Set the **Name** to **ALL**.

Step 3: Update the Code

Next we will want to give our category node a better code to reference it by.

Set the Code to All Products.

Step 4: Update the Description

We can also add a description for the category node.

Set the Description to All Products.

Step 5: Update the Friendly name

Now we will give our top level category node a friendlier name.

Set the Friendly name to All products.

Step 6: Update the Keywords

Finally we can add some keywords to the node for reference.

Set the **Keywords** to **All**.

Step 7: Select the ALL node and click New category node

Now we will want to create a new sub category beneath the **ALL** category.

Select the parent category and click on the **New category node** button.

Step 8: Update the Name

Now we can start configuring the new child category node to expand out our hierarchy.

Set the **Name** to **Indirect**.

Step 9: Update the Code

We will give our new node a unique code to reference it with.

Set the Code to Indirect Products.

Step 10: Update the Description

We will then want to add a description for the new node.

Set the Description to Indirect Products.

 www.dynamicscompanions.com
Dynamics Companions

- 19 -

www.blindsquirrelpublishing.com
© 2019 Blind Squirrel Publishing, LLC, All Rights Reserved

BLIND SQUIRREL
PUBLISHING

DYNAMICS COMPANIONS
BARE BONES CONFIGURATION GUIDE

CONFIGURING PROCUREMENT AND SOURCING WITHIN DYNAMICS 365 FOR FINANCE & OPERATIONS
MODULE 2: CONFIGURING PROCUREMENT CATEGORIES

Step 11: Update the Friendly name

We will continue the setup by giving our new node a friendlier name.

Set the Friendly name to Indirect Products.

Step 12: Update the Keywords

And we will finish off by adding some keywords for the category node.

Set the Keywords to Indirect.

Step 13: Select ALL and click New category node

Now we will want to set up another category node beneath the top category.

Select the **ALL** category node and click on the **New category node** button.

Step 14: Update the Name

We will repeat the process of configuring the category node and start off by changing the name of the node.

Set the **Name** to **Direct**.

Step 15: Update the Code

We will then give the node a unique code to reference it.

Set the Code to Direct Products.

Step 16: Update the Description

We will then add a description to the category node.

Set the Description to Direct Products.

Step 17: Update the Friendly name

We will then give our new node a friendlier name to display to the users.

Set the Friendly name to Direct products.

Step 18: Update the Keywords

And to finish off we will add some keywords for the category node for search purposes.

Set the Keywords to Direct.

Step 19: Select Indirect and click New category node

Now that we have set up the first level of our category hierarchy we will start working on the next level of category nodes.

Select the **Indirect** category node and click on the **New category node** button.

Step 20: Update the Name

Let's change the name of the node to something a little more useful.

Set the Name to Facilities.

Step 21: Update the Code

Next we will want to give the node a unique code to reference it by.

Set the Code to Facilities Magmt.

Step 22: Update the Description

Then we will want to add a description to the category node.

Set the Description to Facilities Management.

Step 23: Update the Friendly name

Then we will want to add a friendlier name to the category node..

Set the Friendly name to Facilities Management.

Step 24: Update the Keywords

And to finish the record off we will add a keyword or two to the new category node.

Set the Keywords to Facilities.

 www.dynamicscompanions.com
Dynamics Companions

- 20 -

www.blindsquirrelpublishing.com
© 2019 Blind Squirrel Publishing, LLC , All Rights Reserved

BLIND SQUIRREL
PUBLISHING

DYNAMICS COMPANIONS
BARE BONES CONFIGURATION GUIDE

CONFIGURING PROCUREMENT AND SOURCING WITHIN DYNAMICS 365 FOR FINANCE & OPERATIONS
MODULE 2: CONFIGURING PROCUREMENT CATEGORIES

Step 25: Select Indirect, click New category node, update the Name, update the Code, update the Description, update the Friendly name and update the Keywords

Let's continue adding nodes to the Category hierarchy and add another Indirect category node.

Select the Indirect node, click on the New category node button, set the Name to Information Technology, set the Code to Information Tech, set the Description to Information Technology, set the Friendly name to Information Technology and set the Keywords to Information Technology.

Step 26: Select Indirect, click New category node, update the Name, update the Code, update the Description, update the Friendly name and update the Keywords

We will continue to add more nodes to the category hierarchy by creating an indirect category for Professional Services.

Select the Indirect node, click on the New category node button, set the Name to Professional Services, set the Code to Profesional Svcs, set the Description to Professional Services, set the Friendly name to Professional Services and set the Keywords to Professional Services.

Step 27: Select Indirect, click New category node, update the Name, update the Code, update the Description, update the Friendly name and update the Keywords

Select the Indirect node, click on the New category node button, set the Name to Marketing, set the Code to Marketing Services, set the Description to Marketing Services, set the Friendly name to Marketing Services and set the Keywords to Marketing Services.

Step 28: Select Indirect, click New category node, update the Name, update the Code, update the Description, update the Friendly name and update the Keywords

Select the Indirect node, click on the New category node button, set the Name to Travel, set the Code to Travel Services, set the Description to Travel Services, set the Friendly name to Travel Services and set the Keywords to Travel Services.

Step 29: Select Indirect, click New category node, update the Name, update the Code, update the Description, update the Friendly name and update the Keywords

Let's add another category node for indirect HR services.

Select the **Indirect** node, click on the **New category node** button, set the **Name** to **HR**, set the **Code** to **HR Services**, set the **Description** to **HR Services**, set the **Friendly name** to **HR Services** and set the **Keywords** to **HR**.

Step 30: Select Indirect, click New category node, update the Name, update the Code, update the Description, update the Friendly name and update the Keywords

Next we will add a category for indirect office supplies.

Select the Indirect node, click on the New category node button, set the Name to Office Supplies, set the Code to Office Supplies, set the Description to Office Supplies, set the Friendly name to Office Supplies and set the Keywords to Office Supplies.

Step 31: Select Indirect, click New category node, update the Name, update the Code,

dync
www.dynamicscompanions.com
Dynamics Companions

- 21 -

www.blindsquirrelpublishing.com
© 2019 Blind Squirrel Publishing, LLC , All Rights Reserved

BLIND SQUIRREL
PUBLISHING

DYNAMICS COMPANIONS
BARE BONES CONFIGURATION GUIDE

CONFIGURING PROCUREMENT AND SOURCING WITHIN DYNAMICS 365 FOR FINANCE & OPERATIONS
MODULE 2: CONFIGURING PROCUREMENT CATEGORIES

update the Description, update the Friendly name and update the Keywords

And we will finish off the indirect categories by adding a node for MRO items.

Select the Indirect node, click on the New category node button, set the Name to MRO, set the Code to MRO, set the Description to Maintenance Repair Operations, set the Friendly name to Maintenance Repair Operations and set the Keywords to Maintenance Repair Operations.

Step 32: Select Direct, click New category node, update the Name, update the Code, update the Description, update the Friendly name and update the Keywords

Now we will add some category nodes to the Direct group in the tree.

Select the Direct node, click on the New category node button, set the Name to Components, set the Code to Components, set the Description to Components, set the Friendly name to Components and set the Keywords to Components.

Step 33: Select Components, click New category node, update the Name, update

the Code, update the Description, update the Friendly name and update the Keywords

We can create as many levels to the hierarchy as we like. To prove this lets add a child node for transistors to the Components node.

Select the Components node, click on the New category node button, set the Name to Transistors, set the Code to Transistors, set the Description to Transistors, set the Friendly name to Transistors and set the Keywords to Transistors.

Step 34: Click Components, click New category node, update the Name, update the Code, update the Description, update the Friendly name and update the Keywords

And we will add another child level to the Components for LED's.

Click on the **Components** button, click on the **New category node** button, set the **Name** to **LEDs**, set the **Code** to **LEDs**, set the **Description** to **LEDs**, set the **Friendly name** to **LEDs** and set the **Keywords** to **LEDs**.

We can keep on adding as many different levels that we like to the Category Hierarchy.

DYNAMICS COMPANIONS
BARE BONES CONFIGURATION GUIDE

CONFIGURING PROCUREMENT AND SOURCING WITHIN DYNAMICS 365 FOR FINANCE & OPERATIONS
MODULE 2: CONFIGURING PROCUREMENT CATEGORIES

Creating a Top Level Procurement Category Node

How to do it...

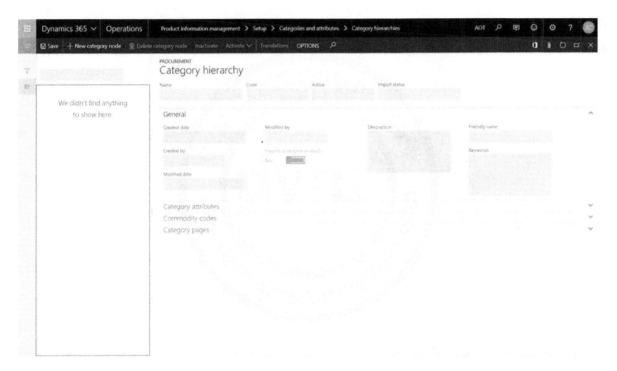

Step 1: Click New

At this point we will want to add our first Category Hierarchy node.

To do this just click on the **New** button.

www.dynamicscompanions.com
Dynamics Companions

- 23 -

www.blindsquirrelpublishing.com
© 2019 Blind Squirrel Publishing, LLC , All Rights Reserved

BLIND SQUIRREL
PUBLISHING

DYNAMICS COMPANIONS
BARE BONES CONFIGURATION GUIDE

CONFIGURING PROCUREMENT AND SOURCING WITHIN DYNAMICS 365 FOR FINANCE & OPERATIONS
MODULE 2: CONFIGURING PROCUREMENT CATEGORIES

Creating a Top Level Procurement Category Node

How to do it...

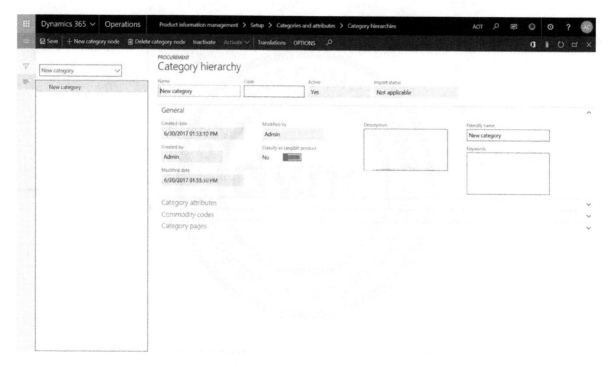

Step 1: Click New

This will create a new category for us within the category designer.

DYNAMICS COMPANIONS
BARE BONES CONFIGURATION GUIDE

CONFIGURING PROCUREMENT AND SOURCING WITHIN DYNAMICS 365 FOR FINANCE & OPERATIONS
MODULE 2: CONFIGURING PROCUREMENT CATEGORIES

Creating a Top Level Procurement Category Node

How to do it...

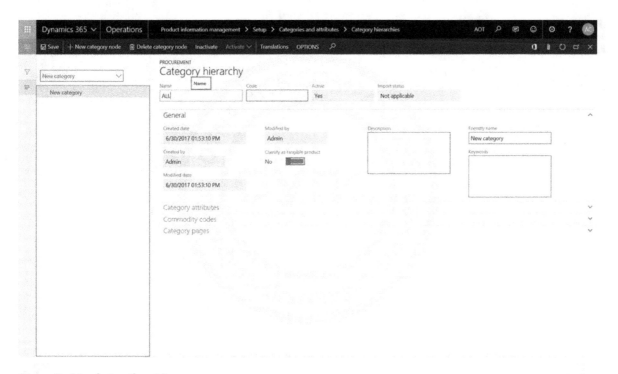

Step 2: Update the Name

Now we will want to rename the Category hierarchy

To do this we will just need to update the **Name** value.

For this example, we will want to set the **Name** to **ALL**.

www.dynamicscompanions.com
Dynamics Companions

- 25 -

www.blindsquirrelpublishing.com
© 2019 Blind Squirrel Publishing, LLC , All Rights Reserved

BLIND SQUIRREL
PUBLISHING

DYNAMICS COMPANIONS
BARE BONES CONFIGURATION GUIDE

CONFIGURING PROCUREMENT AND SOURCING WITHIN DYNAMICS 365 FOR FINANCE & OPERATIONS
MODULE 2: CONFIGURING PROCUREMENT CATEGORIES

Creating a Top Level Procurement Category Node

How to do it...

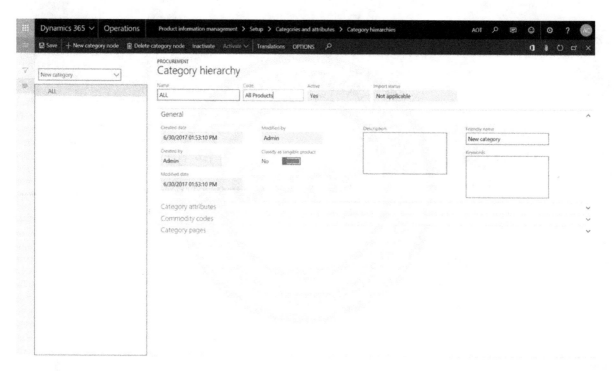

Step 3: Update the Code

Next we will want to give our category node a better code to reference it by.

To do this we will just need to update the **Code** value.

For this example, we will want to set the **Code** to **All Products**.

www.dynamicscompanions.com
Dynamics Companions

- 26 -

www.blindsquirrelpublishing.com
© 2019 Blind Squirrel Publishing, LLC , All Rights Reserved

BLIND SQUIRREL
PUBLISHING

DYNAMICS COMPANIONS
BARE BONES CONFIGURATION GUIDE

CONFIGURING PROCUREMENT AND SOURCING WITHIN DYNAMICS 365 FOR FINANCE & OPERATIONS
MODULE 2: CONFIGURING PROCUREMENT CATEGORIES

Creating a Top Level Procurement Category Node

How to do it...

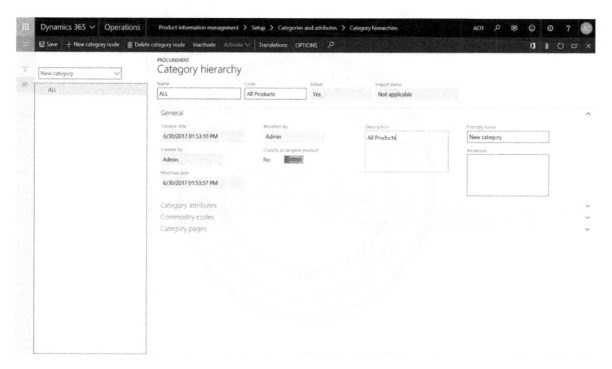

Step 4: Update the Description

We can also add a description for the category node.

To do this we will just need to update the **Description** value.

For this example, we will want to set the **Description** to **All Products**.

dync
www.dynamicscompanions.com
Dynamics Companions

- 27 -

www.blindsquirrelpublishing.com
© 2019 Blind Squirrel Publishing, LLC, All Rights Reserved

BLIND SQUIRREL
PUBLISHING

DYNAMICS COMPANIONS
BARE BONES CONFIGURATION GUIDE

CONFIGURING PROCUREMENT AND SOURCING WITHIN DYNAMICS 365 FOR FINANCE & OPERATIONS
MODULE 2: CONFIGURING PROCUREMENT CATEGORIES

Creating a Top Level Procurement Category Node

How to do it...

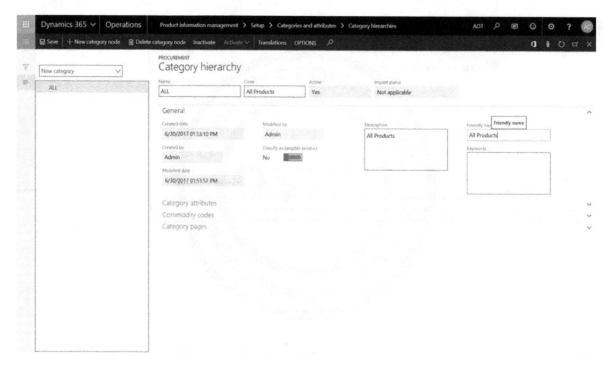

Step 5: Update the Friendly name

Now we will give our top level category node a friendlier name.

To do this we will just need to update the **Friendly name** value.

For this example, we will want to set the **Friendly name** to **All products**.

dyn c
www.dynamicscompanions.com
Dynamics Companions

- 28 -

www.blindsquirrelpublishing.com
© 2019 Blind Squirrel Publishing, LLC , All Rights Reserved

BLIND SQUIRREL
PUBLISHING

DYNAMICS COMPANIONS
BARE BONES CONFIGURATION GUIDE

CONFIGURING PROCUREMENT AND SOURCING WITHIN DYNAMICS 365 FOR FINANCE & OPERATIONS
MODULE 2: CONFIGURING PROCUREMENT CATEGORIES

Creating a Top Level Procurement Category Node

How to do it...

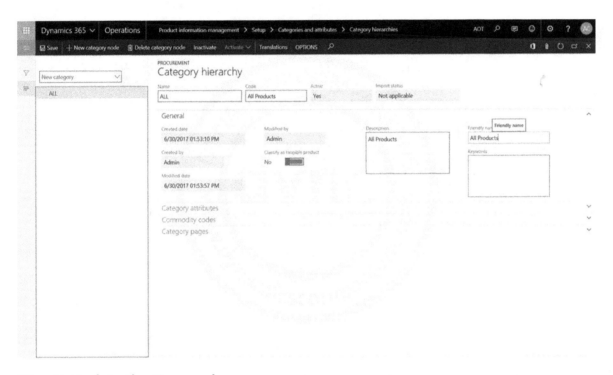

Step 6: Update the Keywords

Finally we can add some keywords to the node for reference.

To do this we will just need to update the **Keywords** value.

For this example, we will want to set the **Keywords** to **All**.

dyn c
www.dynamicscompanions.com
Dynamics Companions

- 29 -

www.blindsquirrelpublishing.com
© 2019 Blind Squirrel Publishing, LLC, All Rights Reserved

BLIND SQUIRREL
PUBLISHING

DYNAMICS COMPANIONS
BARE BONES CONFIGURATION GUIDE

CONFIGURING PROCUREMENT AND SOURCING WITHIN DYNAMICS 365 FOR FINANCE & OPERATIONS
MODULE 2: CONFIGURING PROCUREMENT CATEGORIES

Creating a Top Level Procurement Category Node

How to do it...

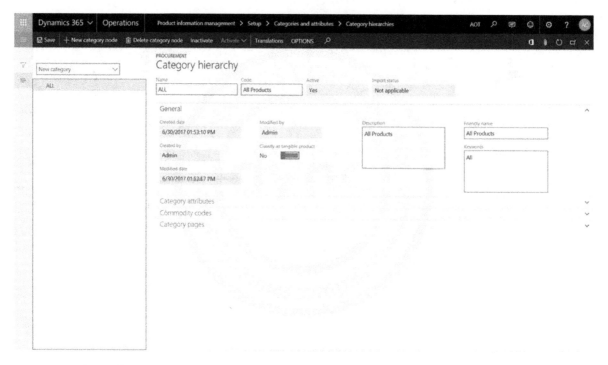

Step 7: Select the ALL node and click New category node

Now we will want to create a new sub category beneath the **ALL** category.

To do this just select the parent node and then click on the **New category node** button.

For this example we selected the **ALL** category node and then clicked on the **New category node** button.

dync
www.dynamicscompanions.com
Dynamics Companions

- 30 -

www.blindsquirrelpublishing.com
© 2019 Blind Squirrel Publishing, LLC , All Rights Reserved

BLIND SQUIRREL
PUBLISHING

DYNAMICS COMPANIONS
BARE BONES CONFIGURATION GUIDE

CONFIGURING PROCUREMENT AND SOURCING WITHIN DYNAMICS 365 FOR FINANCE & OPERATIONS
MODULE 2: CONFIGURING PROCUREMENT CATEGORIES

Creating a Top Level Procurement Category Node

How to do it...

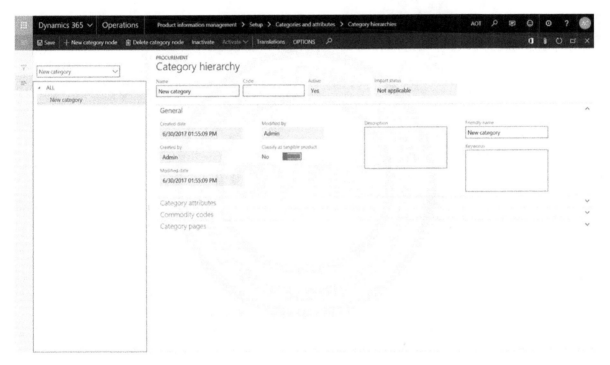

Step 7: Select the ALL node and click New category node

This will create a new child node for us below the **ALL** category node.

dyn⊂
www.dynamicscompanions.com
Dynamics Companions

- 31 -

www.blindsquirrelpublishing.com
© 2019 Blind Squirrel Publishing, LLC , All Rights Reserved

BLIND SQUIRREL
PUBLISHING

DYNAMICS COMPANIONS
BARE BONES CONFIGURATION GUIDE

CONFIGURING PROCUREMENT AND SOURCING WITHIN DYNAMICS 365 FOR FINANCE & OPERATIONS
MODULE 2: CONFIGURING PROCUREMENT CATEGORIES

Creating a Top Level Procurement Category Node

How to do it...

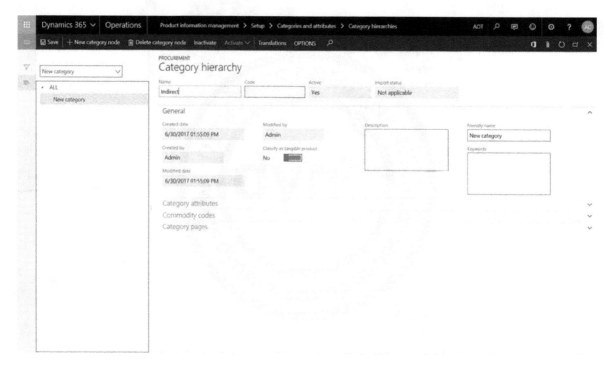

Step 8: Update the Name

Now we can start configuring the new child category node to expand out our hierarchy.

To do this we will just need to update the **Name** value.

For this example, we will want to set the **Name** to **Indirect**.

dyn c
dynamics companions
www.dynamicscompanions.com
Dynamics Companions

- 32 -

www.blindsquirrelpublishing.com
© 2019 Blind Squirrel Publishing, LLC , All Rights Reserved

BLIND SQUIRREL
PUBLISHING

DYNAMICS COMPANIONS
BARE BONES CONFIGURATION GUIDE

CONFIGURING PROCUREMENT AND SOURCING WITHIN DYNAMICS 365 FOR FINANCE & OPERATIONS
MODULE 2: CONFIGURING PROCUREMENT CATEGORIES

Creating a Top Level Procurement Category Node

How to do it...

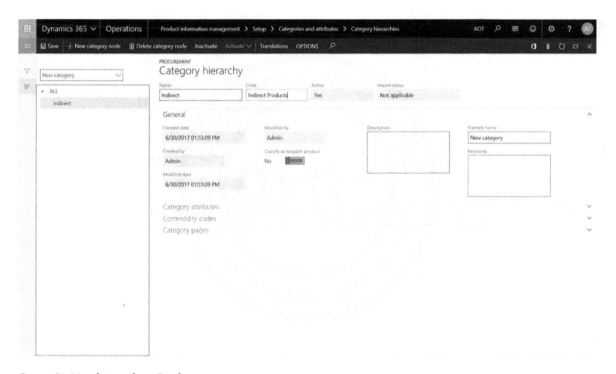

Step 9: Update the Code

We will give our new node a unique code to reference it with.

To do this we will just need to update the **Code** value.

For this example, we will want to set the **Code** to **Indirect Products**.

dync
www.dynamicscompanions.com
Dynamics Companions

- 33 -

www.blindsquirrelpublishing.com
© 2019 Blind Squirrel Publishing, LLC , All Rights Reserved

BLIND SQUIRREL
PUBLISHING

DYNAMICS COMPANIONS
BARE BONES CONFIGURATION GUIDE

CONFIGURING PROCUREMENT AND SOURCING WITHIN DYNAMICS 365 FOR FINANCE & OPERATIONS
MODULE 2: CONFIGURING PROCUREMENT CATEGORIES

Creating a Top Level Procurement Category Node

How to do it...

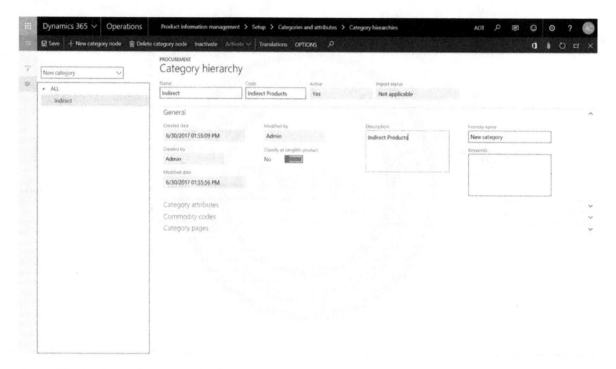

Step 10: Update the Description

We will then want to add a description for the new node.

To do this we will just need to update the **Description** value.

For this example, we will want to set the **Description** to **Indirect Products**.

DYNAMICS COMPANIONS
BARE BONES CONFIGURATION GUIDE

CONFIGURING PROCUREMENT AND SOURCING WITHIN DYNAMICS 365 FOR FINANCE & OPERATIONS
MODULE 2: CONFIGURING PROCUREMENT CATEGORIES

Creating a Top Level Procurement Category Node

How to do it...

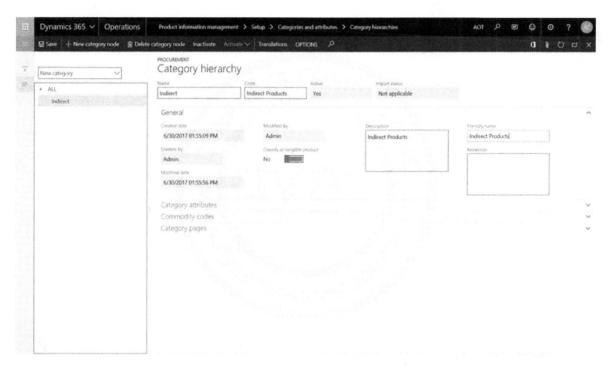

Step 11: Update the Friendly name

We will continue the setup by giving our new node a friendlier name.

To do this we will just need to update the **Friendly name** value.

For this example, we will want to set the **Friendly name** to **Indirect Products**.

dync
www.dynamicscompanions.com
Dynamics Companions

- 35 -

www.blindsquirrelpublishing.com
© 2019 Blind Squirrel Publishing, LLC , All Rights Reserved

BLIND SQUIRREL
PUBLISHING

DYNAMICS COMPANIONS
BARE BONES CONFIGURATION GUIDE

CONFIGURING PROCUREMENT AND SOURCING WITHIN DYNAMICS 365 FOR FINANCE & OPERATIONS
MODULE 2: CONFIGURING PROCUREMENT CATEGORIES

Creating a Top Level Procurement Category Node

How to do it...

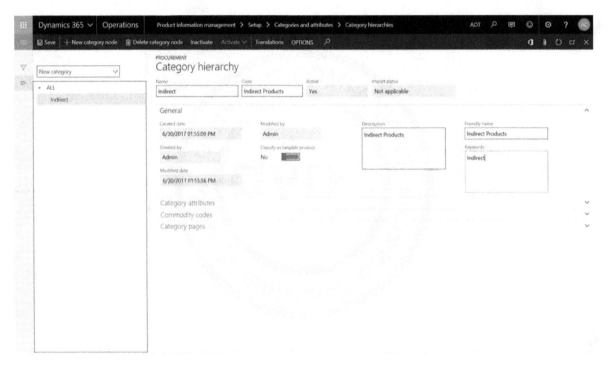

Step 12: Update the Keywords

And we will finish off by adding some keywords for the category node.

To do this we will just need to update the **Keywords** value.

For this example, we will want to set the **Keywords** to **Indirect**.

dyn c
www.dynamicscompanions.com
Dynamics Companions

- 36 -

www.blindsquirrelpublishing.com
© 2019 Blind Squirrel Publishing, LLC , All Rights Reserved

BLIND SQUIRREL
PUBLISHING

DYNAMICS COMPANIONS
BARE BONES CONFIGURATION GUIDE

CONFIGURING PROCUREMENT AND SOURCING WITHIN DYNAMICS 365 FOR FINANCE & OPERATIONS
MODULE 2: CONFIGURING PROCUREMENT CATEGORIES

Creating a Top Level Procurement Category Node

How to do it...

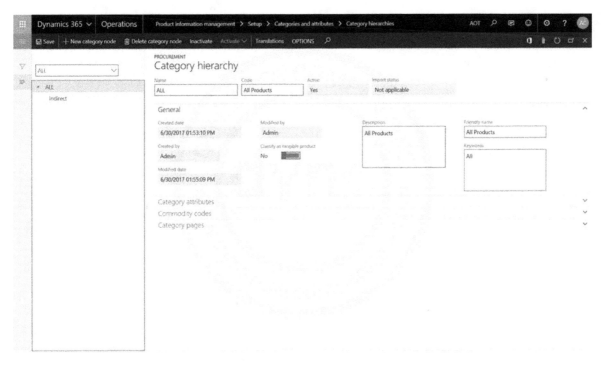

Step 13: Select ALL and click New category node

Now we will want to set up another category node beneath the top category.

To do this just select the **ALL** category node and click on the **New category node** button.

DYNAMICS COMPANIONS
BARE BONES CONFIGURATION GUIDE

CONFIGURING PROCUREMENT AND SOURCING WITHIN DYNAMICS 365 FOR FINANCE & OPERATIONS
MODULE 2: CONFIGURING PROCUREMENT CATEGORIES

Creating a Top Level Procurement Category Node

How to do it...

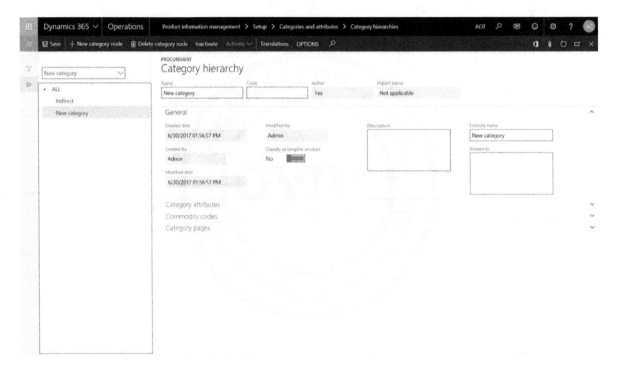

Step 13: Select ALL and click New category node

This will create a new node for us to configure.

www.dynamicscompanions.com
Dynamics Companions

- 38 -

www.blindsquirrelpublishing.com
© 2019 Blind Squirrel Publishing, LLC, All Rights Reserved

BLIND SQUIRREL
PUBLISHING

DYNAMICS COMPANIONS
BARE BONES CONFIGURATION GUIDE

CONFIGURING PROCUREMENT AND SOURCING WITHIN DYNAMICS 365 FOR FINANCE & OPERATIONS
MODULE 2: CONFIGURING PROCUREMENT CATEGORIES

Creating a Top Level Procurement Category Node

How to do it...

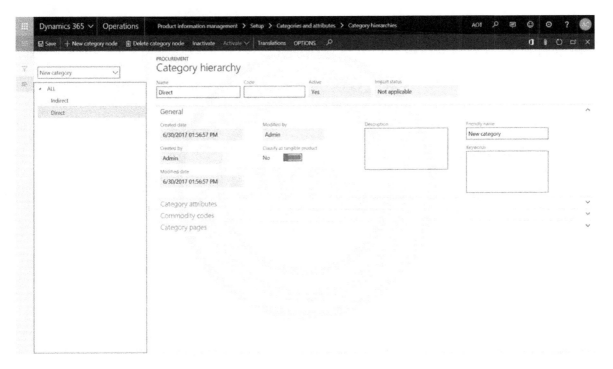

Step 14: Update the Name

We will repeat the process of configuring the category node and start off by changing the name of the node.

To do this we will just need to update the **Name** value.

For this example, we will want to set the **Name** to **Direct**.

dync
www.dynamicscompanions.com
Dynamics Companions

- 39 -

www.blindsquirrelpublishing.com
© 2019 Blind Squirrel Publishing, LLC, All Rights Reserved

BLIND SQUIRREL
PUBLISHING

DYNAMICS COMPANIONS
BARE BONES CONFIGURATION GUIDE

CONFIGURING PROCUREMENT AND SOURCING WITHIN DYNAMICS 365 FOR FINANCE & OPERATIONS
MODULE 2: CONFIGURING PROCUREMENT CATEGORIES

Creating a Top Level Procurement Category Node

How to do it...

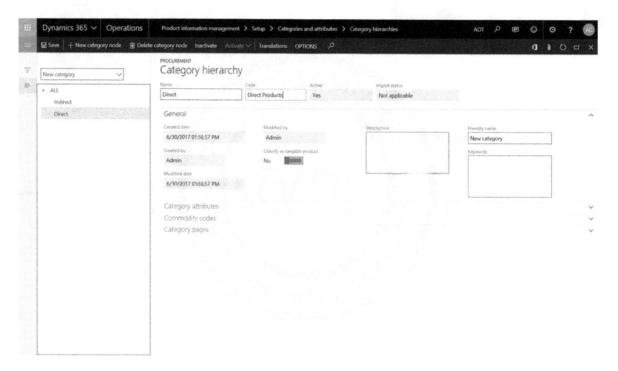

Step 15: Update the Code

We will then give the node a unique code to reference it.

To do this we will just need to update the **Code** value.

For this example, we will want to set the **Code** to **Direct Products**.

dyn c
www.dynamicscompanions.com
Dynamics Companions

- 40 -

www.blindsquirrelpublishing.com
© 2019 Blind Squirrel Publishing, LLC , All Rights Reserved

BLIND SQUIRREL
PUBLISHING

DYNAMICS COMPANIONS
BARE BONES CONFIGURATION GUIDE

CONFIGURING PROCUREMENT AND SOURCING WITHIN DYNAMICS 365 FOR FINANCE & OPERATIONS
MODULE 2: CONFIGURING PROCUREMENT CATEGORIES

Creating a Top Level Procurement Category Node

How to do it...

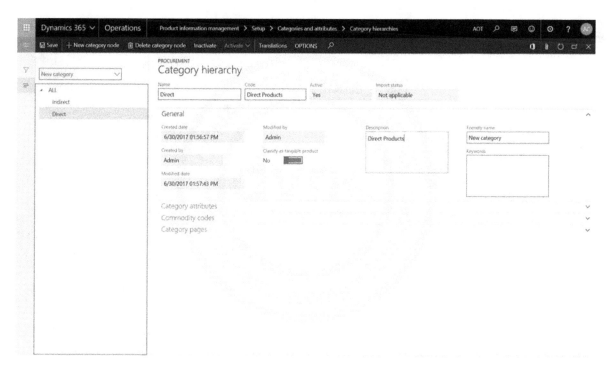

Step 16: Update the Description

We will then add a description to the category node.

To do this we will just need to update the **Description** value.

For this example, we will want to set the **Description** to **Direct Products**.

dyn c
www.dynamicscompanions.com
Dynamics Companions

- 41 -

www.blindsquirrelpublishing.com
© 2019 Blind Squirrel Publishing, LLC , All Rights Reserved

BLIND SQUIRREL
PUBLISHING

DYNAMICS COMPANIONS
BARE BONES CONFIGURATION GUIDE

CONFIGURING PROCUREMENT AND SOURCING WITHIN DYNAMICS 365 FOR FINANCE & OPERATIONS
MODULE 2: CONFIGURING PROCUREMENT CATEGORIES

Creating a Top Level Procurement Category Node

How to do it...

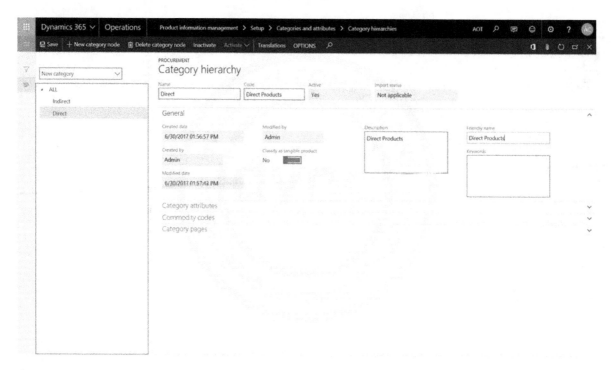

Step 17: Update the Friendly name

We will then give our new node a friendlier name to display to the users.

To do this we will just need to update the **Friendly name** value.

For this example, we will want to set the **Friendly name** to **Direct products**.

dyn c
www.dynamicscompanions.com
Dynamics Companions

- 42 -

www.blindsquirrelpublishing.com
© 2019 Blind Squirrel Publishing, LLC, All Rights Reserved

BLIND SQUIRREL
PUBLISHING

DYNAMICS COMPANIONS
BARE BONES CONFIGURATION GUIDE

CONFIGURING PROCUREMENT AND SOURCING WITHIN DYNAMICS 365 FOR FINANCE & OPERATIONS
MODULE 2: CONFIGURING PROCUREMENT CATEGORIES

Creating a Top Level Procurement Category Node

How to do it...

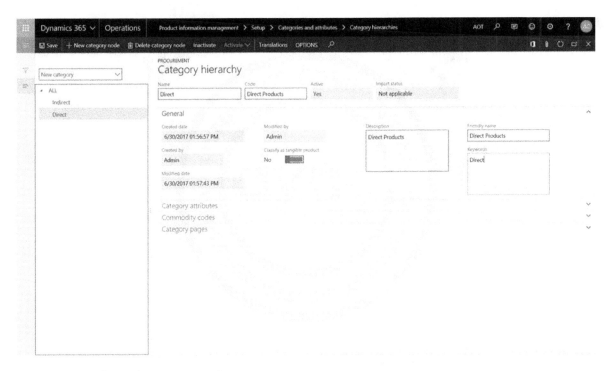

Step 18: Update the Keywords

And to finish off we will add some keywords for the category node for search purposes.

To do this we will just need to update the **Keywords** value.

For this example, we will want to set the **Keywords** to **Direct**.

dyn c
www.dynamicscompanions.com
Dynamics Companions

- 43 -

www.blindsquirrelpublishing.com
© 2019 Blind Squirrel Publishing, LLC, All Rights Reserved

BLIND SQUIRREL
PUBLISHING

DYNAMICS COMPANIONS
BARE BONES CONFIGURATION GUIDE

CONFIGURING PROCUREMENT AND SOURCING WITHIN DYNAMICS 365 FOR FINANCE & OPERATIONS
MODULE 2: CONFIGURING PROCUREMENT CATEGORIES

Creating a Top Level Procurement Category Node

How to do it...

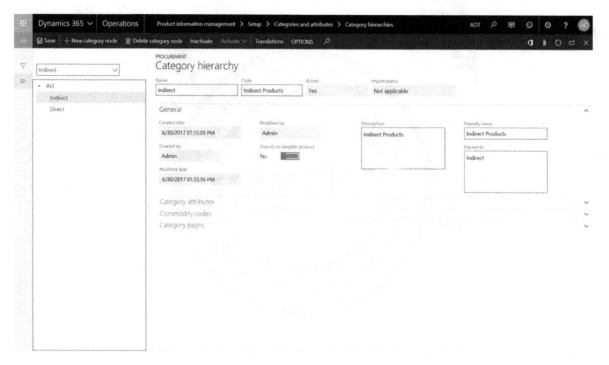

Step 19: Select Indirect and click New category node

Now that we have set up the first level of our category hierarchy we will start working on the next level of category nodes.

To do this just select the **Indirect** category node and click on the **New category node** button.

dyn c
www.dynamicscompanions.com
Dynamics Companions

- 44 -

www.blindsquirrelpublishing.com
© 2019 Blind Squirrel Publishing, LLC , All Rights Reserved

BLIND SQUIRREL
PUBLISHING

DYNAMICS COMPANIONS
BARE BONES CONFIGURATION GUIDE

CONFIGURING PROCUREMENT AND SOURCING WITHIN DYNAMICS 365 FOR FINANCE & OPERATIONS
MODULE 2: CONFIGURING PROCUREMENT CATEGORIES

Creating a Top Level Procurement Category Node

How to do it...

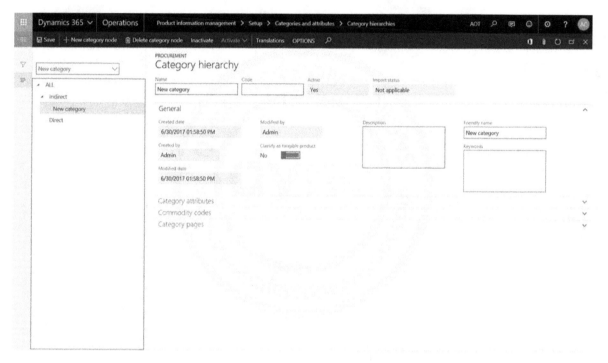

Step 19: Select Indirect and click New category node

Now you will have a category below the **Indirect** category.

This will create a new category node for us under the Indirect category node.

www.dynamicscompanions.com
Dynamics Companions

- 45 -

www.blindsquirrelpublishing.com
© 2019 Blind Squirrel Publishing, LLC , All Rights Reserved

BLIND SQUIRREL
PUBLISHING

DYNAMICS COMPANIONS
BARE BONES CONFIGURATION GUIDE

CONFIGURING PROCUREMENT AND SOURCING WITHIN DYNAMICS 365 FOR FINANCE & OPERATIONS
MODULE 2: CONFIGURING PROCUREMENT CATEGORIES

Creating a Top Level Procurement Category Node

How to do it...

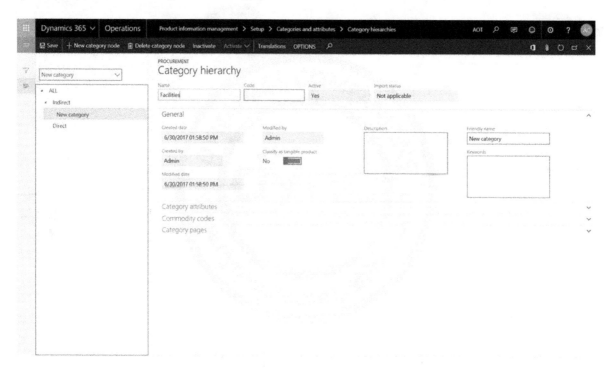

Step 20: Update the Name

Let's change the name of the node to something a little more useful.

Dynamics 365 for Finance and Operations, Financials Functional Consultant AssociateFor this example, we will want to set the **Name** to **Facilities**.

dync
www.dynamicscompanions.com
Dynamics Companions

- 46 -

www.blindsquirrelpublishing.com
© 2019 Blind Squirrel Publishing, LLC , All Rights Reserved

BLIND SQUIRREL
PUBLISHING

DYNAMICS COMPANIONS
BARE BONES CONFIGURATION GUIDE

CONFIGURING PROCUREMENT AND SOURCING WITHIN DYNAMICS 365 FOR FINANCE & OPERATIONS
MODULE 2: CONFIGURING PROCUREMENT CATEGORIES

Creating a Top Level Procurement Category Node

How to do it...

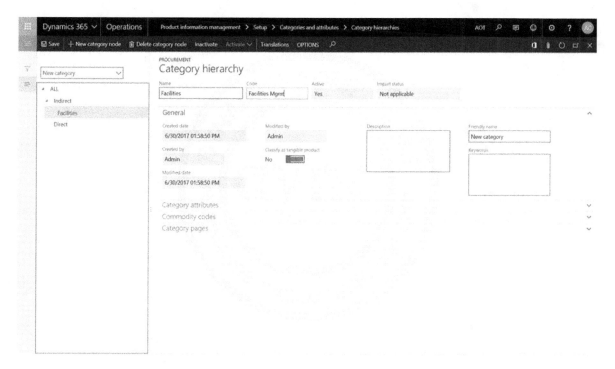

Step 21: Update the Code

Next we will want to give the node a unique code to reference it by.

To do this we will just need to update the **Code** value.

For this example, we will want to set the **Code** to **Facilities Magmt**.

dync

www.dynamicscompanions.com
Dynamics Companions

- 47 -

www.blindsquirrelpublishing.com
© 2019 Blind Squirrel Publishing, LLC, All Rights Reserved

BLIND SQUIRREL
PUBLISHING

DYNAMICS COMPANIONS
BARE BONES CONFIGURATION GUIDE

CONFIGURING PROCUREMENT AND SOURCING WITHIN DYNAMICS 365 FOR FINANCE & OPERATIONS
MODULE 2: CONFIGURING PROCUREMENT CATEGORIES

Creating a Top Level Procurement Category Node

How to do it...

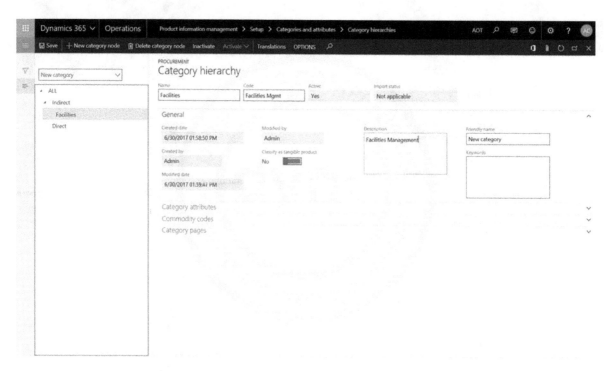

Step 22: Update the Description

Then we will want to add a description to the category node.

To do this we will just need to update the **Description** value.

For this example, we will want to set the **Description** to **Facilities Management**.

www.dynamicscompanions.com
Dynamics Companions

- 48 -

www.blindsquirrelpublishing.com
© 2019 Blind Squirrel Publishing, LLC , All Rights Reserved

BLIND SQUIRREL
PUBLISHING

DYNAMICS COMPANIONS
BARE BONES CONFIGURATION GUIDE

CONFIGURING PROCUREMENT AND SOURCING WITHIN DYNAMICS 365 FOR FINANCE & OPERATIONS
MODULE 2: CONFIGURING PROCUREMENT CATEGORIES

Creating a Top Level Procurement Category Node

How to do it...

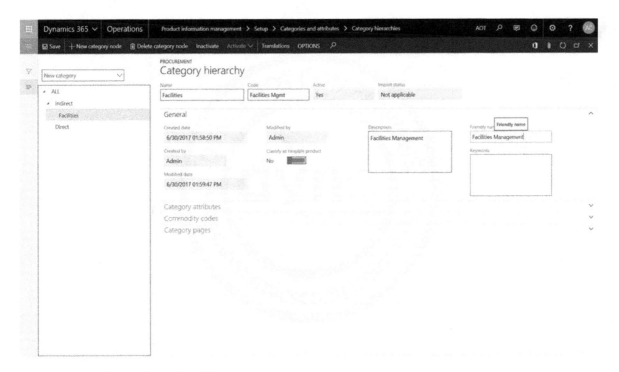

Step 23: Update the Friendly name

Then we will want to add a friendlier name to the category node..

To do this we will just need to update the **Friendly name** value.

For this example, we will want to set the **Friendly name** to **Facilities Management**.

dync
www.dynamicscompanions.com
Dynamics Companions

- 49 -

www.blindsquirrelpublishing.com
© 2019 Blind Squirrel Publishing, LLC, All Rights Reserved

BLIND SQUIRREL
PUBLISHING

DYNAMICS COMPANIONS
BARE BONES CONFIGURATION GUIDE

CONFIGURING PROCUREMENT AND SOURCING WITHIN DYNAMICS 365 FOR FINANCE & OPERATIONS
MODULE 2: CONFIGURING PROCUREMENT CATEGORIES

Creating a Top Level Procurement Category Node

How to do it...

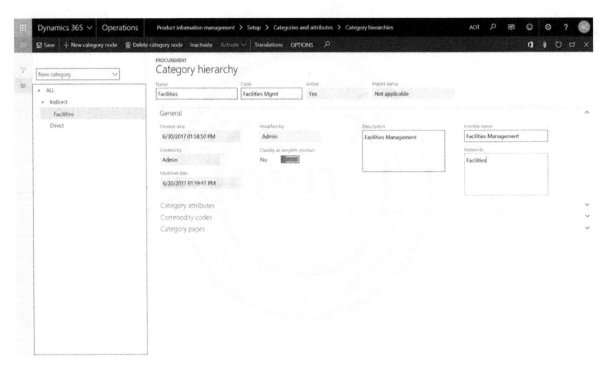

Step 24: Update the Keywords

And to finish the record off we will add a keyword or two to the new category node.

To do this we will just need to update the **Keywords** value.

For this example, we will want to set the **Keywords** to **Facilities**.

dyn c
www.dynamicscompanions.com
Dynamics Companions

- 50 -

www.blindsquirrelpublishing.com
© 2019 Blind Squirrel Publishing, LLC , All Rights Reserved

BLIND SQUIRREL
PUBLISHING

DYNAMICS COMPANIONS
BARE BONES CONFIGURATION GUIDE

CONFIGURING PROCUREMENT AND SOURCING WITHIN DYNAMICS 365 FOR FINANCE & OPERATIONS
MODULE 2: CONFIGURING PROCUREMENT CATEGORIES

Creating a Top Level Procurement Category Node

How to do it...

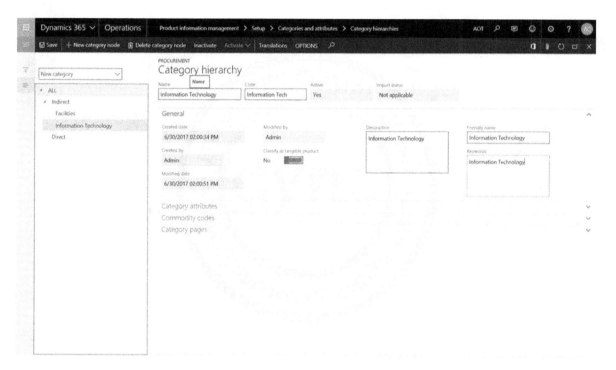

Step 25: Select Indirect, click New category node, update the Name, update the Code, update the Description, update the Friendly name and update the Keywords

Let's continue adding nodes to the Category hierarchy and add another Indirect category node.

To do this just select the **Indirect** node, click on the **New category node** button, update the **Name** value, update the **Code** value, update the **Description** value, update the **Friendly name** value and update the **Keywords** value.

For this example, we will want to set the Name to Information Technology, set the Code to Information Tech, set the Description to Information Technology, set the Friendly name to Information Technology and set the Keywords to Information Technology.

dyn c
www.dynamicscompanions.com
Dynamics Companions

- 51 -

www.blindsquirrelpublishing.com
© 2019 Blind Squirrel Publishing, LLC , All Rights Reserved

BLIND SQUIRREL
PUBLISHING

DYNAMICS COMPANIONS
BARE BONES CONFIGURATION GUIDE

CONFIGURING PROCUREMENT AND SOURCING WITHIN DYNAMICS 365 FOR FINANCE & OPERATIONS
MODULE 2: CONFIGURING PROCUREMENT CATEGORIES

Creating a Top Level Procurement Category Node

How to do it...

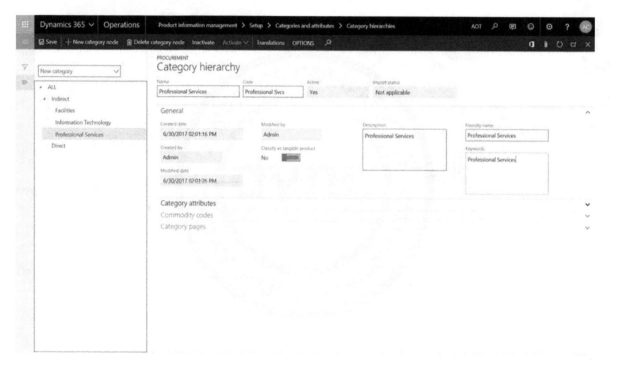

Step 26: Select Indirect, click New category node, update the Name, update the Code, update the Description, update the Friendly name and update the Keywords

We will continue to add more nodes to the category hierarchy by creating an indirect category for Professional Services.

To do this just select the **Indirect** node, click on the **New category node** button, update the **Name** value, update the **Code** value, update the **Description** value, update the **Friendly name** value and update the **Keywords** value.

For this example, we will want to set the Name to Professional Services, set the Code to Profesional Svcs, set the Description to Professional Services, set the Friendly name to Professional Services and set the Keywords to Professional Services.

dyn c
www.dynamicscompanions.com
Dynamics Companions

- 52 -

www.blindsquirrelpublishing.com
© 2019 Blind Squirrel Publishing, LLC , All Rights Reserved

BLIND SQUIRREL
PUBLISHING

DYNAMICS COMPANIONS
BARE BONES CONFIGURATION GUIDE

CONFIGURING PROCUREMENT AND SOURCING WITHIN DYNAMICS 365 FOR FINANCE & OPERATIONS
MODULE 2: CONFIGURING PROCUREMENT CATEGORIES

Creating a Top Level Procurement Category Node

How to do it...

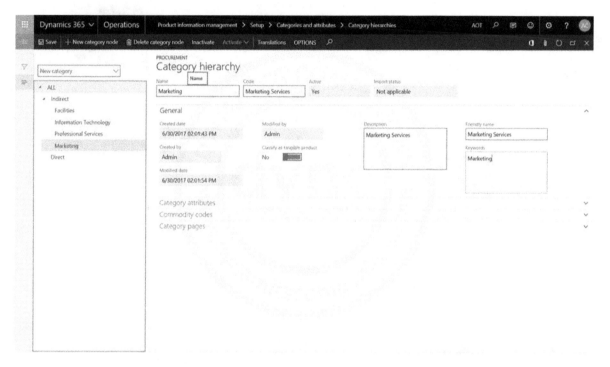

Step 27: Select Indirect, click New category node, update the Name, update the Code, update the Description, update the Friendly name and update the Keywords

To do this just select the **Indirect** node, click on the **New category node** button, update the **Name** value, update the **Code** value, update the **Description** value, update the **Friendly name** value and update the **Keywords** value.

For this example, we will want to set the Name to Marketing, set the Code to Marketing Services, set the Description to Marketing Services, set the Friendly name to Marketing Services and set the Keywords to Marketing Services.

dyn c
www.dynamicscompanions.com
Dynamics Companions
- 53 -
www.blindsquirrelpublishing.com
© 2019 Blind Squirrel Publishing, LLC , All Rights Reserved
BLIND SQUIRREL
PUBLISHING

DYNAMICS COMPANIONS
BARE BONES CONFIGURATION GUIDE

CONFIGURING PROCUREMENT AND SOURCING WITHIN DYNAMICS 365 FOR FINANCE & OPERATIONS
MODULE 2: CONFIGURING PROCUREMENT CATEGORIES

Creating a Top Level Procurement Category Node

How to do it...

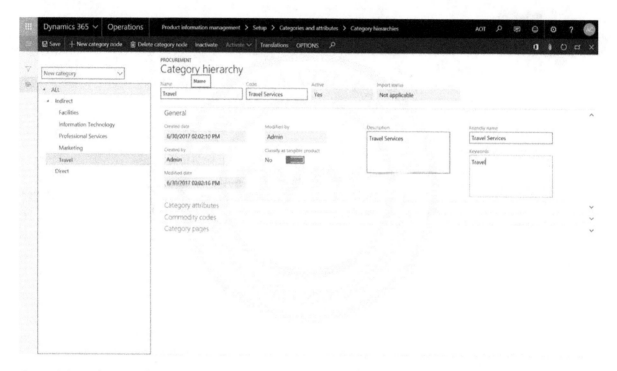

Step 28: Select Indirect, click New category node, update the Name, update the Code, update the Description, update the Friendly name and update the Keywords

To do this just select the **Indirect** category node, click on the **New category node** button, update the **Name** value, update the **Code** value, update the **Description** value, update the **Friendly name** value and update the **Keywords** value.

For this example, we will want to set the **Name** to **Travel**, set the **Code** to **Travel Services**, set the **Description** to **Travel Services**, set the **Friendly name** to **Travel Services** and set the **Keywords** to **Travel Services**.

dync
www.dynamicscompanions.com
Dynamics Companions

- 54 -

www.blindsquirrelpublishing.com
© 2019 Blind Squirrel Publishing, LLC , All Rights Reserved

BLIND SQUIRREL
PUBLISHING

DYNAMICS COMPANIONS
BARE BONES CONFIGURATION GUIDE

CONFIGURING PROCUREMENT AND SOURCING WITHIN DYNAMICS 365 FOR FINANCE & OPERATIONS
MODULE 2: CONFIGURING PROCUREMENT CATEGORIES

Creating a Top Level Procurement Category Node

How to do it...

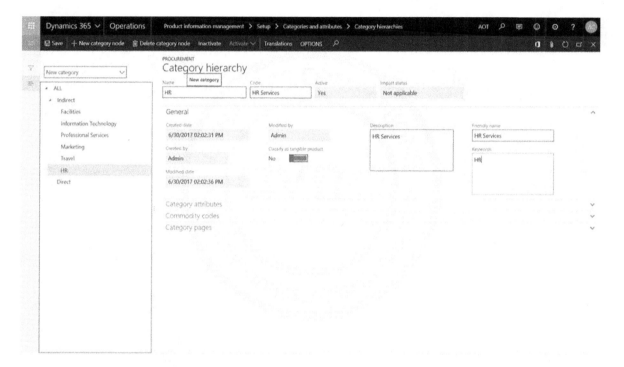

Step 29: Select Indirect, click New category node, update the Name, update the Code, update the Description, update the Friendly name and update the Keywords

Let's add another category node for indirect HR services.

To do this just select the **Indirect** node, click on the **New category node** button, update the **Name** value, update the **Code** value, update the **Description** value, update the **Friendly name** value and update the **Keywords** value.

For this example, we will want to set the **Name** to **HR**, set the **Code** to **HR Services**, set the **Description** to **HR Services**, set the **Friendly name** to **HR Services** and set the **Keywords** to **HR**.

dyn c
www.dynamicscompanions.com
Dynamics Companions

- 55 -

www.blindsquirrelpublishing.com
© 2019 Blind Squirrel Publishing, LLC , All Rights Reserved

BLIND SQUIRREL
PUBLISHING

DYNAMICS COMPANIONS
BARE BONES CONFIGURATION GUIDE

CONFIGURING PROCUREMENT AND SOURCING WITHIN DYNAMICS 365 FOR FINANCE & OPERATIONS
MODULE 2: CONFIGURING PROCUREMENT CATEGORIES

Creating a Top Level Procurement Category Node

How to do it...

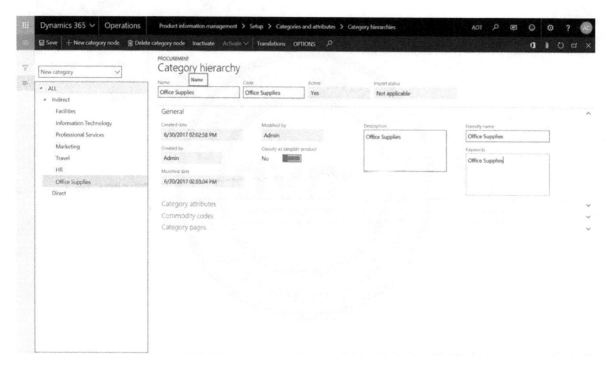

Step 30: Select Indirect, click New category node, update the Name, update the Code, update the Description, update the Friendly name and update the Keywords

Next we will add a category for indirect office supplies.

To do this just select the **Indirect** node, click on the **New category node** button, update the **Name** value, update the **Code** value, update the **Description** value, update the **Friendly name** value and update the **Keywords** value.

For this example, we will want to set the Name to Office Supplies, set the Code to Office Supplies, set the Description to Office Supplies, set the Friendly name to Office Supplies and set the Keywords to Office Supplies.

dync
www.dynamicscompanions.com
Dynamics Companions

- 56 -

www.blindsquirrelpublishing.com
© 2019 Blind Squirrel Publishing, LLC , All Rights Reserved

BLIND SQUIRREL
PUBLISHING

DYNAMICS COMPANIONS
BARE BONES CONFIGURATION GUIDE

CONFIGURING PROCUREMENT AND SOURCING WITHIN DYNAMICS 365 FOR FINANCE & OPERATIONS
MODULE 2: CONFIGURING PROCUREMENT CATEGORIES

Creating a Top Level Procurement Category Node

How to do it...

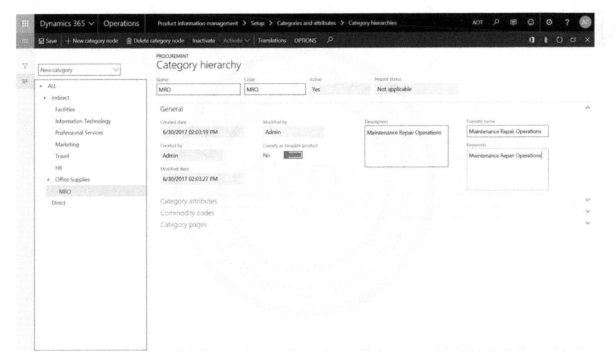

Step 31: Select Indirect, click New category node, update the Name, update the Code, update the Description, update the Friendly name and update the Keywords

And we will finish off the indirect categories by adding a node for MRO items.

To do this just select the **Indirect** node, click on the **New category node** button, update the **Name** value, update the **Code** value, update the **Description** value, update the **Friendly name** value and update the **Keywords** value.

For this example, we will want to set the Name to MRO, set the Code to MRO, set the Description to Maintenance Repair Operations, set the Friendly name to Maintenance Repair Operations and set the Keywords to Maintenance Repair Operations.

dync
www.dynamicscompanions.com
Dynamics Companions

- 57 -

www.blindsquirrelpublishing.com
© 2019 Blind Squirrel Publishing, LLC, All Rights Reserved

BLIND SQUIRREL
PUBLISHING

DYNAMICS COMPANIONS
BARE BONES CONFIGURATION GUIDE

CONFIGURING PROCUREMENT AND SOURCING WITHIN DYNAMICS 365 FOR FINANCE & OPERATIONS
MODULE 2: CONFIGURING PROCUREMENT CATEGORIES

Creating a Top Level Procurement Category Node

How to do it...

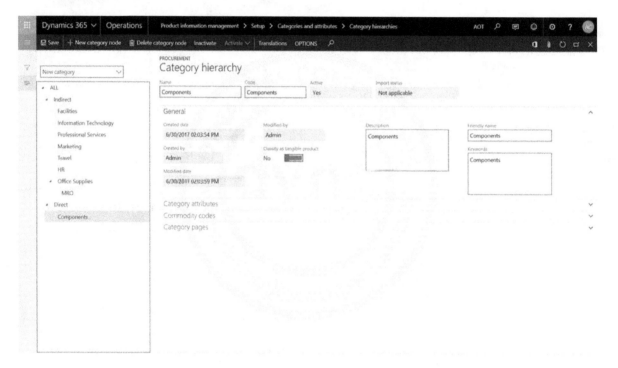

Step 32: Select Direct, click New category node, update the Name, update the Code, update the Description, update the Friendly name and update the Keywords

Now we will add some category nodes to the Direct group in the tree.

To do this just select the **Direct** node, click on the **New category node** button, update the **Name** value, update the **Code** value, update the **Description** value, update the **Friendly name** value and update the **Keywords** value.

For this example, we will want to set the **Name** to **Components**, set the **Code** to **Components**, set the **Description** to **Components**, set the **Friendly name** to **Components** and set the **Keywords** to **Components**.

www.dynamicscompanions.com
Dynamics Companions

- 58 -

www.blindsquirrelpublishing.com
© 2019 Blind Squirrel Publishing, LLC , All Rights Reserved

BLIND SQUIRREL
PUBLISHING

DYNAMICS COMPANIONS
BARE BONES CONFIGURATION GUIDE

CONFIGURING PROCUREMENT AND SOURCING WITHIN DYNAMICS 365 FOR FINANCE & OPERATIONS
MODULE 2: CONFIGURING PROCUREMENT CATEGORIES

Creating a Top Level Procurement Category Node

How to do it...

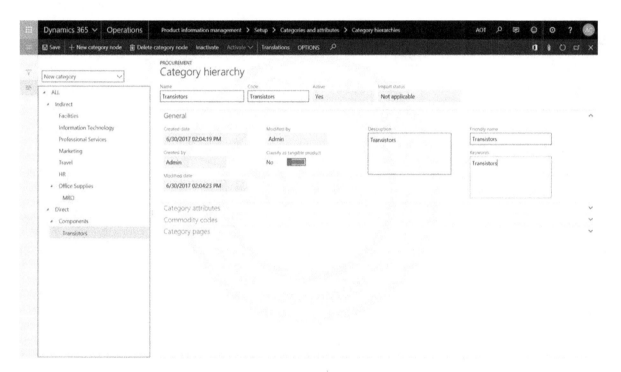

Step 33: Select Components, click New category node, update the Name, update the Code, update the Description, update the Friendly name and update the Keywords

We can create as many levels to the hierarchy as we like. To prove this lets add a child node for transistors to the Components node.

To do this just select the **Components** node, click on the **New category node** button, update the **Name** value, update the **Code** value, update the **Description** value, update the **Friendly name** value and update the **Keywords** value.

For this example, we will want to set the **Name** to **Transistors**, set the **Code** to **Transistors**, set the **Description** to **Transistors**, set the **Friendly name** to **Transistors** and set the **Keywords** to **Transistors**.

dyn c

www.dynamicscompanions.com
Dynamics Companions

- 59 -

www.blindsquirrelpublishing.com
© 2019 Blind Squirrel Publishing, LLC , All Rights Reserved

BLIND SQUIRREL
PUBLISHING

DYNAMICS COMPANIONS
BARE BONES CONFIGURATION GUIDE

CONFIGURING PROCUREMENT AND SOURCING WITHIN DYNAMICS 365 FOR FINANCE & OPERATIONS
MODULE 2: CONFIGURING PROCUREMENT CATEGORIES

Creating a Top Level Procurement Category Node

How to do it...

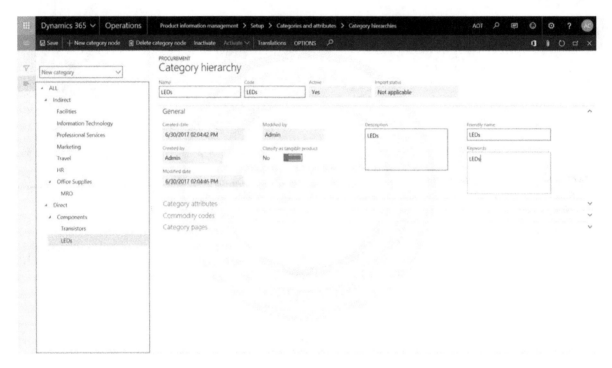

Step 34: Click Components, click New category node, update the Name, update the Code, update the Description, update the Friendly name and update the Keywords

And we will add another child level to the Components for LED's.

To do this just click on the **Components** button, click on the **New category node** button, update the **Name** value, update the **Code** value, update the **Description** value, update the **Friendly name** value and update the **Keywords** value.

For this example, we will want to set the **Name** to **LEDs**, set the **Code** to **LEDs**, set the **Description** to **LEDs**, set the **Friendly name** to **LEDs** and set the **Keywords** to **LEDs**.

dyn c
dynamics companions
www.dynamicscompanions.com
Dynamics Companions

- 60 -

www.blindsquirrelpublishing.com
© 2019 Blind Squirrel Publishing, LLC , All Rights Reserved

BLIND SQUIRREL
PUBLISHING

DYNAMICS COMPANIONS
BARE BONES CONFIGURATION GUIDE

CONFIGURING PROCUREMENT AND SOURCING WITHIN DYNAMICS 365 FOR FINANCE & OPERATIONS
MODULE 2: CONFIGURING PROCUREMENT CATEGORIES

Creating a Top Level Procurement Category Node

How to do it...

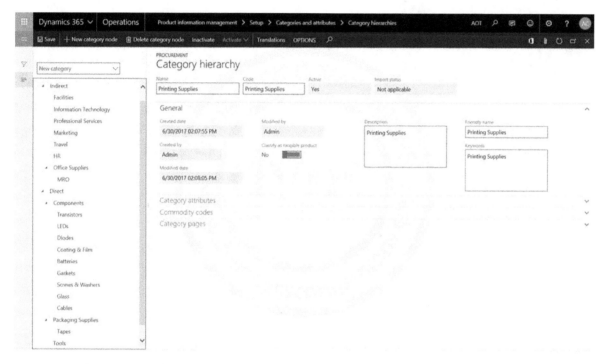

Step 34: Click Components, click New category node, update the Name, update the Code, update the Description, update the Friendly name and update the Keywords

We can keep on adding as many different levels that we like to the Category Hierarchy.

Examples could be

Components
  Transistors
  LEDs
  Diodes
  Coating & Films Batteries
  Gaskets
  Screws & Washers
  Glass
  Cables
  Encoders
Packaging Supplies
  Tapes

www.dynamicscompanions.com
Dynamics Companions

- 61 -

www.blindsquirrelpublishing.com
© 2019 Blind Squirrel Publishing, LLC , All Rights Reserved

BLIND SQUIRREL
PUBLISHING

DYNAMICS COMPANIONS
BARE BONES CONFIGURATION GUIDE

CONFIGURING PROCUREMENT AND SOURCING WITHIN DYNAMICS 365 FOR FINANCE & OPERATIONS
MODULE 2: CONFIGURING PROCUREMENT CATEGORIES

Tools
Printing Supplies
  Toner

After you are done, click on the **Close** button to exit from the form.

www.dynamicscompanions.com
Dynamics Companions

- 62 -

www.blindsquirrelpublishing.com
© 2019 Blind Squirrel Publishing, LLC , All Rights Reserved

BLIND SQUIRREL
PUBLISHING

DYNAMICS COMPANIONS
BARE BONES CONFIGURATION GUIDE

CONFIGURING PROCUREMENT AND SOURCING WITHIN DYNAMICS 365 FOR FINANCE & OPERATIONS
MODULE 2: CONFIGURING PROCUREMENT CATEGORIES

Configuring Category Hierarchy Types

Next we want to link the **Category Hierarchy** that we just created to the **Procurement & Sourcing** module so that we can use it to set up the purchasing details.

How to do it...

Step 1: Open the Category hierarchy role associations form through the menu

We can get to the **Category hierarchy role associations** form a couple of different ways. The first way is through the master menu.

Navigate to Product Information Management > Setup > Categories and attributes > Category hierarchy role associations.

Step 2: Open the Category hierarchy role associations form through the menu search

Another way that we can find the **Category hierarchy role associations** form is through the menu search feature.

Type in category heir r into the menu search and select Category hierarchy role associations.

Step 3: Click New

We will want to create a new role association record.

Click on the **New** button.

Step 4: Select the Category hierarchy type

We will now want to select the type of Category hierarchy that we are associating to this role.

Click on the Category hierarchy type dropdown list and select Procurement category hierarchy.

Step 5: Select the Category hierarchy

This will then allow us to select our new Category hierarchy that we just created.

Click on the **Category hierarchy** dropdown list and select **Procurement**.

www.dynamicscompanions.com
Dynamics Companions

- 63 -

www.blindsquirrelpublishing.com
© 2019 Blind Squirrel Publishing, LLC , All Rights Reserved

BLIND SQUIRREL
PUBLISHING

DYNAMICS COMPANIONS
BARE BONES CONFIGURATION GUIDE

CONFIGURING PROCUREMENT AND SOURCING WITHIN DYNAMICS 365 FOR FINANCE & OPERATIONS
MODULE 2: CONFIGURING PROCUREMENT CATEGORIES

Configuring Category Hierarchy Types

How to do it...

Step 1: Open the Category hierarchy role associations form through the menu

We can get to the **Category hierarchy role associations** form a couple of different ways. The first way is through the master menu.

To do this, open up the navigation panel, expand out the **Modules** and group, and click on **Product Information Management** to see all of the menu items that are available. Then click on the **Category hierarchy role associations** menu item within the **Categories and attributes** folder of the **Setup** group.

www.dynamicscompanions.com
Dynamics Companions

- 64 -

www.blindsquirrelpublishing.com
© 2019 Blind Squirrel Publishing, LLC , All Rights Reserved

BLIND SQUIRREL
PUBLISHING

DYNAMICS COMPANIONS
BARE BONES CONFIGURATION GUIDE

CONFIGURING PROCUREMENT AND SOURCING WITHIN DYNAMICS 365 FOR FINANCE & OPERATIONS
MODULE 2: CONFIGURING PROCUREMENT CATEGORIES

Configuring Category Hierarchy Types

How to do it...

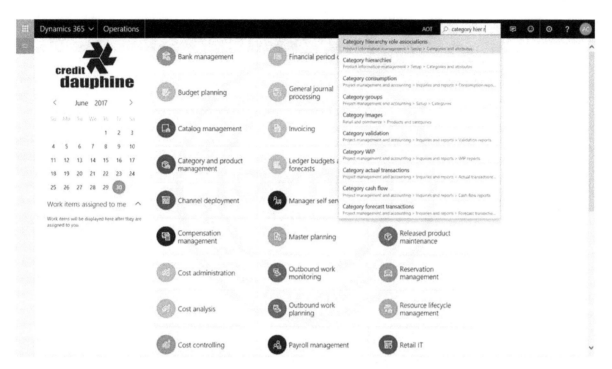

Step 2: Open the Category hierarchy role associations form through the menu search

Another way that we can find the **Category hierarchy role associations** form is through the menu search feature.

dyn c
Dynamics Companions

www.dynamicscompanions.com
Dynamics Companions

- 65 -

www.blindsquirrelpublishing.com
© 2019 Blind Squirrel Publishing, LLC , All Rights Reserved

BLIND SQUIRREL
PUBLISHING

DYNAMICS COMPANIONS
BARE BONES CONFIGURATION GUIDE

CONFIGURING PROCUREMENT AND SOURCING WITHIN DYNAMICS 365 FOR FINANCE & OPERATIONS
MODULE 2: CONFIGURING PROCUREMENT CATEGORIES

Configuring Category Hierarchy Types

How to do it...

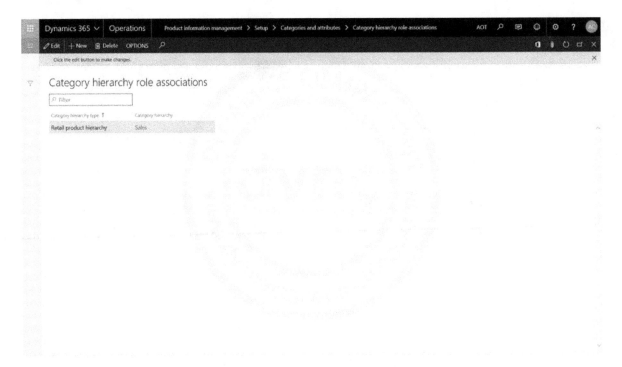

Step 2: Open the Category hierarchy role associations form through the menu search

This will open up the **Category hierarchy role associations** maintenance form where we will be able to set up our procurement category hierarchy as the default Procurement hierarchy.

dyn c
www.dynamicscompanions.com
Dynamics Companions

- 66 -

www.blindsquirrelpublishing.com
© 2019 Blind Squirrel Publishing, LLC, All Rights Reserved

BLIND SQUIRREL
PUBLISHING

DYNAMICS COMPANIONS
BARE BONES CONFIGURATION GUIDE

CONFIGURING PROCUREMENT AND SOURCING WITHIN DYNAMICS 365 FOR FINANCE & OPERATIONS
MODULE 2: CONFIGURING PROCUREMENT CATEGORIES

Configuring Category Hierarchy Types

How to do it...

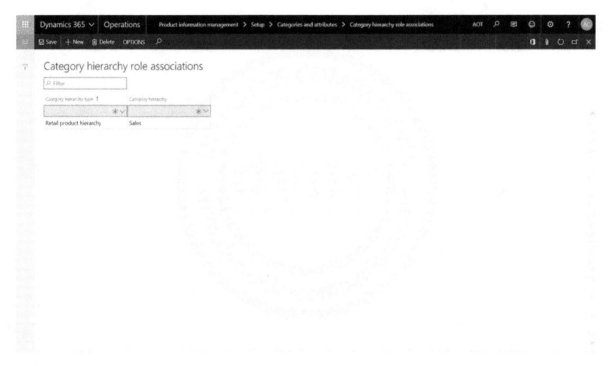

Step 3: Click New

We will want to create a new role association record.

To do this just click on the **New** button.

www.dynamicscompanions.com
Dynamics Companions

- 67 -

www.blindsquirrelpublishing.com
© 2019 Blind Squirrel Publishing, LLC , All Rights Reserved

BLIND SQUIRREL
PUBLISHING

DYNAMICS COMPANIONS
BARE BONES CONFIGURATION GUIDE

CONFIGURING PROCUREMENT AND SOURCING WITHIN DYNAMICS 365 FOR FINANCE & OPERATIONS
MODULE 2: CONFIGURING PROCUREMENT CATEGORIES

Configuring Category Hierarchy Types

How to do it...

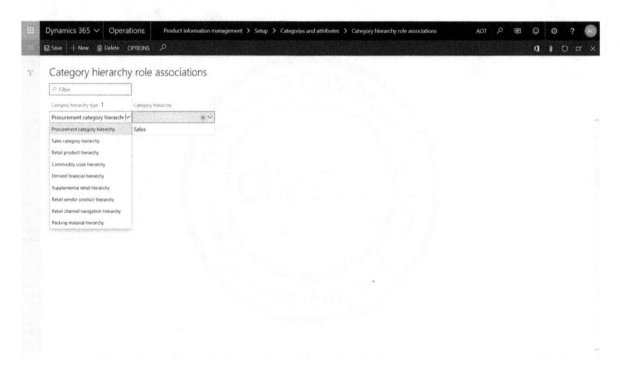

Step 4: Select the Category hierarchy type

We will now want to select the type of Category hierarchy that we are associating to this role.

To do this we will just need to select the **Category hierarchy type** from the dropdown list.

For this example, we will want to click on the **Category hierarchy type** dropdown list and select **Procurement category hierarchy**.

dyn c   www.dynamicscompanions.com
Dynamics Companions

- 68 -

www.blindsquirrelpublishing.com
© 2019 Blind Squirrel Publishing, LLC , All Rights Reserved

BLIND SQUIRREL
PUBLISHING

DYNAMICS COMPANIONS
BARE BONES CONFIGURATION GUIDE

CONFIGURING PROCUREMENT AND SOURCING WITHIN DYNAMICS 365 FOR FINANCE & OPERATIONS
MODULE 2: CONFIGURING PROCUREMENT CATEGORIES

Configuring Category Hierarchy Types

How to do it...

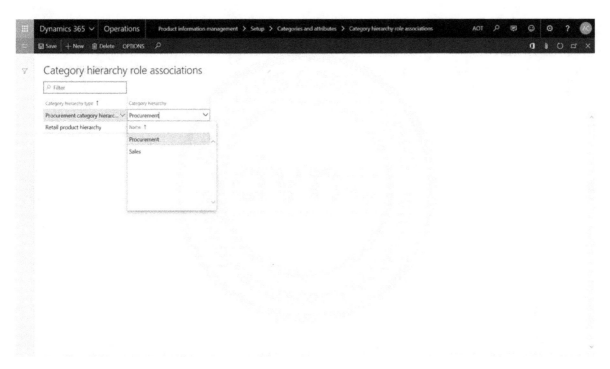

Step 5: Select the Category hierarchy

This will then allow us to select our new Category hierarchy that we just created.

To do this we will just need to select the **Category hierarchy** from the dropdown list.

For this example, we will want to click on the **Category hierarchy** dropdown list and select **Procurement**.

dync
Dynamics Companions

www.dynamicscompanions.com
Dynamics Companions

- 69 -

www.blindsquirrelpublishing.com
© 2019 Blind Squirrel Publishing, LLC, All Rights Reserved

BLIND SQUIRREL
PUBLISHING

DYNAMICS COMPANIONS
BARE BONES CONFIGURATION GUIDE

CONFIGURING PROCUREMENT AND SOURCING WITHIN DYNAMICS 365 FOR FINANCE & OPERATIONS
MODULE 2: CONFIGURING PROCUREMENT CATEGORIES

Configuring Category Hierarchy Types

How to do it...

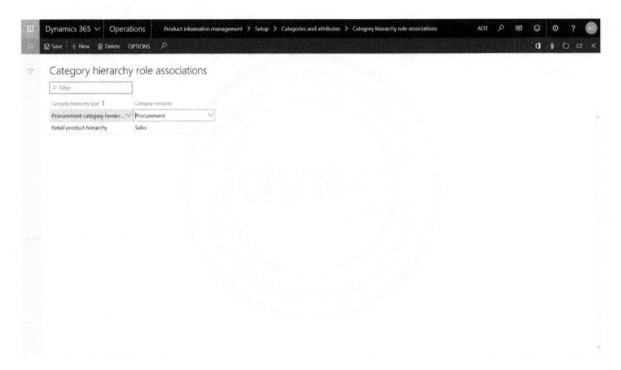

Step 5: Select the Category hierarchy

After you have done that click on the **Close** button to exit from the form.

dyn c
www.dynamicscompanions.com
Dynamics Companions

- 70 -

www.blindsquirrelpublishing.com
© 2019 Blind Squirrel Publishing, LLC , All Rights Reserved

BLIND SQUIRREL
PUBLISHING

DYNAMICS COMPANIONS
BARE BONES CONFIGURATION GUIDE

CONFIGURING PROCUREMENT AND SOURCING WITHIN DYNAMICS 365 FOR FINANCE & OPERATIONS
MODULE 2: CONFIGURING PROCUREMENT CATEGORIES

Assigning Products To Procurement Categories

Now that we have built our **Procurement Categories**, we can start assigning our products to them for the procurement processes.

How to do it...

Step 1: Open the Procurement categories form through the menu

We can get to the **Procurement categories** form a couple of different ways. The first way is through the master menu.

Navigate to Procurement and sourcing > Procurement categories.

Step 2: Open the Procurement categories form through the menu search

Another way that we can find the **Procurement categories** form is through the menu search feature.

Type in **procurement cate** into the menu search and select **Procurement categories**.

Step 3: Select Transistors

Now we will want to start adding our products to the categories. We will start off by choosing the category that we want to add them to.

Select the **Transistors** node.

Step 4: Expand Products

Now that we are in the category we will see that there are a lot of fast tabs that we can configure data in. The on that we are

interested in is the one that has all of the products associated with it.

Expand the **Products** fast tab.

Step 5: Click Add

This will allow us to see the list of products that are in this category. Right now the cupboards are a little bare.

Now we will add some products to the category.

Click on the **Add** button.

Step 6: Click Product name filter

There are a lot of products here in the list, so rather than scroll through them all to find the products that we want to use, let's filter out the list of products.

Click on the **Product name** filter.

Step 7: Click contains

All of our transistor products have transistor somewhere in their name. It may not be at the beginning so we will want to change the filter criteria to look through the entire name.

Click on the **contains** button.

DYNAMICS COMPANIONS
BARE BONES CONFIGURATION GUIDE

CONFIGURING PROCUREMENT AND SOURCING WITHIN DYNAMICS 365 FOR FINANCE & OPERATIONS
MODULE 2: CONFIGURING PROCUREMENT CATEGORIES

Step 8: Update the Product name

Now we will want to enter the key word that we want to look for in the name.

Set the Product name to transistor.

Step 9: Selecy 700201 and click ->

We can select products individually and add them to the category.

Select the **700201** record and click on the **->** button.

Step 10: Click Select all and click ->

But there is an easier way to do this, and that is to select all of the filtered products and add them to the category.

Click on the **Select all** button and click on the **->** button.

Step 11: Click OK

This will move all of the products over to the selected panel. After we have done that we can exit from the form.

Click on the **OK** button.

We can repeat the process for all of the other **Procurement Categories**.

www.dynamicscompanions.com
Dynamics Companions

- 72 -

www.blindsquirrelpublishing.com
© 2019 Blind Squirrel Publishing, LLC , All Rights Reserved

DYNAMICS COMPANIONS
BARE BONES CONFIGURATION GUIDE

CONFIGURING PROCUREMENT AND SOURCING WITHIN DYNAMICS 365 FOR FINANCE & OPERATIONS
MODULE 2: CONFIGURING PROCUREMENT CATEGORIES

Assigning Products To Procurement Categories

How to do it...

Step 1: Open the Procurement categories form through the menu

We can get to the **Procurement categories** form a couple of different ways. The first way is through the master menu.

To do this, open up the navigation panel, expand out the **Modules** and group, and click on **Procurement and sourcing** to see all of the menu items that are available. Then click on the **Procurement categories** menu item.

www.dynamicscompanions.com
Dynamics Companions

- 73 -

www.blindsquirrelpublishing.com
© 2019 Blind Squirrel Publishing, LLC , All Rights Reserved

BLIND SQUIRREL
PUBLISHING

DYNAMICS COMPANIONS
BARE BONES CONFIGURATION GUIDE

CONFIGURING PROCUREMENT AND SOURCING WITHIN DYNAMICS 365 FOR FINANCE & OPERATIONS
MODULE 2: CONFIGURING PROCUREMENT CATEGORIES

Assigning Products To Procurement Categories

How to do it...

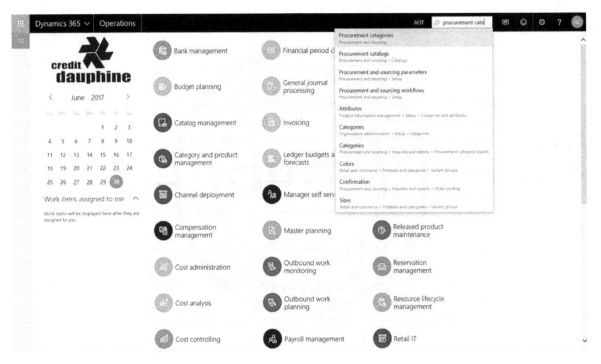

Step 2: Open the Procurement categories form through the menu search

Another way that we can find the **Procurement categories** form is through the menu search feature.

We can do this by clicking on the search icon in the header of the form (or by pressing **ALT+G**) and then type in **procurement cate** storage into the search box. Then you will be able to select the **Procurement categories** form from the dropdown list.

dyn c
www.dynamicscompanions.com
Dynamics Companions

- 74 -

www.blindsquirrelpublishing.com
© 2019 Blind Squirrel Publishing, LLC , All Rights Reserved

BLIND SQUIRREL
PUBLISHING

DYNAMICS COMPANIONS
BARE BONES CONFIGURATION GUIDE

CONFIGURING PROCUREMENT AND SOURCING WITHIN DYNAMICS 365 FOR FINANCE & OPERATIONS
MODULE 2: CONFIGURING PROCUREMENT CATEGORIES

Assigning Products To Procurement Categories

How to do it...

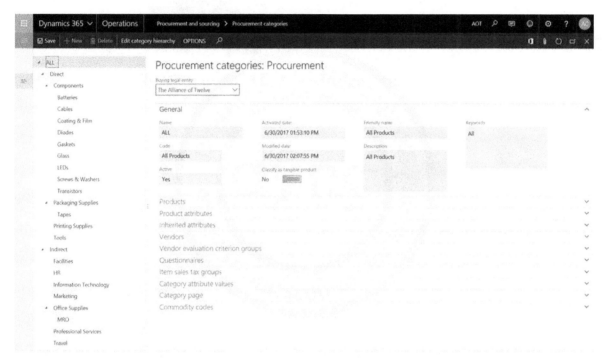

Step 2: Open the Procurement categories form through the menu search

When the **Procurement Categories** maintenance form is displayed, you will see that all of the categories that you set up within the **Category Hierarchy** will be waiting for you.

dyn c

www.dynamicscompanions.com
Dynamics Companions

- 75 -

www.blindsquirrelpublishing.com
© 2019 Blind Squirrel Publishing, LLC , All Rights Reserved

BLIND SQUIRREL
PUBLISHING

DYNAMICS COMPANIONS
BARE BONES CONFIGURATION GUIDE

CONFIGURING PROCUREMENT AND SOURCING WITHIN DYNAMICS 365 FOR FINANCE & OPERATIONS
MODULE 2: CONFIGURING PROCUREMENT CATEGORIES

Assigning Products To Procurement Categories

How to do it...

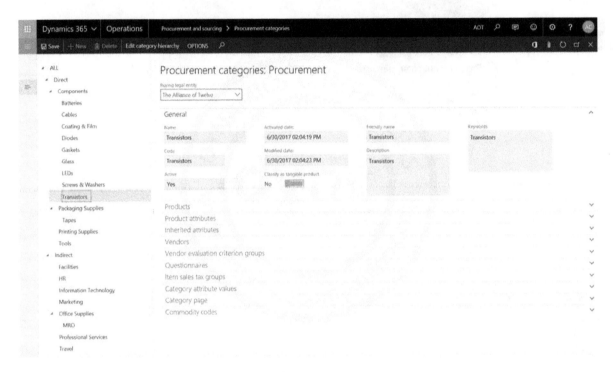

Step 3: Select Transistors

Now we will want to start adding our products to the categories. We will start off by choosing the category that we want to add them to.

To do this just select the **Transistors** node.

www.dynamicscompanions.com
Dynamics Companions

- 76 -

www.blindsquirrelpublishing.com
© 2019 Blind Squirrel Publishing, LLC , All Rights Reserved

BLIND SQUIRREL
PUBLISHING

DYNAMICS COMPANIONS
BARE BONES CONFIGURATION GUIDE

CONFIGURING PROCUREMENT AND SOURCING WITHIN DYNAMICS 365 FOR FINANCE & OPERATIONS
MODULE 2: CONFIGURING PROCUREMENT CATEGORIES

Assigning Products To Procurement Categories

How to do it...

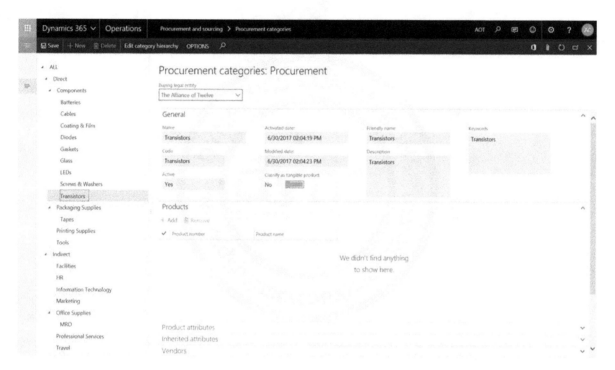

Step 4: Expand Products

Now that we are in the category we will see that there are a lot of fast tabs that we can configure data in. The on that we are interested in is the one that has all of the products associated with it.

To do this just expand the **Products** fast tab.

dync
www.dynamicscompanions.com
Dynamics Companions

- 77 -

www.blindsquirrelpublishing.com
© 2019 Blind Squirrel Publishing, LLC, All Rights Reserved

BLIND SQUIRREL
PUBLISHING

DYNAMICS COMPANIONS
BARE BONES CONFIGURATION GUIDE

CONFIGURING PROCUREMENT AND SOURCING WITHIN DYNAMICS 365 FOR FINANCE & OPERATIONS
MODULE 2: CONFIGURING PROCUREMENT CATEGORIES

Assigning Products To Procurement Categories

How to do it...

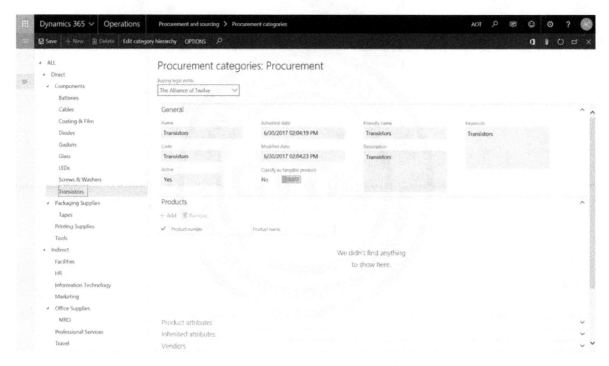

Step 5: Click Add

This will allow us to see the list of products that are in this category. Right now the cupboards are a little bare.

Now we will add some products to the category.

To do this just click on the **Add** button.

dyn c
www.dynamicscompanions.com
Dynamics Companions

- 78 -

www.blindsquirrelpublishing.com
© 2019 Blind Squirrel Publishing, LLC , All Rights Reserved

BLIND SQUIRREL
PUBLISHING

DYNAMICS COMPANIONS
BARE BONES CONFIGURATION GUIDE

CONFIGURING PROCUREMENT AND SOURCING WITHIN DYNAMICS 365 FOR FINANCE & OPERATIONS
MODULE 2: CONFIGURING PROCUREMENT CATEGORIES

Assigning Products To Procurement Categories

How to do it...

Step 5: Click Add

This will open up a list of all the products that you have loaded into the system.

This will open up a selection form where we will be able to see all of our products that are available to us to add to the category and also the ones that have already been selected.

dyn©
www.dynamicscompanions.com
Dynamics Companions

- 79 -

www.blindsquirrelpublishing.com
© 2019 Blind Squirrel Publishing, LLC , All Rights Reserved

BLIND SQUIRREL
PUBLISHING

DYNAMICS COMPANIONS
BARE BONES CONFIGURATION GUIDE

CONFIGURING PROCUREMENT AND SOURCING WITHIN DYNAMICS 365 FOR FINANCE & OPERATIONS
MODULE 2: CONFIGURING PROCUREMENT CATEGORIES

Assigning Products To Procurement Categories

How to do it...

Step 6: Click Product name filter

There are a lot of products here in the list, so rather than scroll through them all to find the products that we want to use, let's filter out the list of products.

To do this just click on the **Product name** filter.

www.dynamicscompanions.com
Dynamics Companions

- 80 -

www.blindsquirrelpublishing.com
© 2019 Blind Squirrel Publishing, LLC , All Rights Reserved

BLIND SQUIRREL
PUBLISHING

DYNAMICS COMPANIONS
BARE BONES CONFIGURATION GUIDE

CONFIGURING PROCUREMENT AND SOURCING WITHIN DYNAMICS 365 FOR FINANCE & OPERATIONS
MODULE 2: CONFIGURING PROCUREMENT CATEGORIES

Assigning Products To Procurement Categories

How to do it...

Step 7: Click contains

All of our transistor products have transistor somewhere in their name. It may not be at the beginning so we will want to change the filter criteria to look through the entire name.

To do this just click on the **contains** button.

www.dynamicscompanions.com
Dynamics Companions

- 81 -

www.blindsquirrelpublishing.com
© 2019 Blind Squirrel Publishing, LLC , All Rights Reserved

BLIND SQUIRREL
PUBLISHING

DYNAMICS COMPANIONS
BARE BONES CONFIGURATION GUIDE

CONFIGURING PROCUREMENT AND SOURCING WITHIN DYNAMICS 365 FOR FINANCE & OPERATIONS
MODULE 2: CONFIGURING PROCUREMENT CATEGORIES

Assigning Products To Procurement Categories

How to do it...

Step 8: Update the Product name

Now we will want to enter the key word that we want to look for in the name.

To do this we will just need to update the **Product name** value.

For this example, we will want to set the **Product name** to **transistor**.

www.dynamicscompanions.com
Dynamics Companions

- 82 -

www.blindsquirrelpublishing.com
© 2019 Blind Squirrel Publishing, LLC , All Rights Reserved

BLIND SQUIRREL
PUBLISHING

DYNAMICS COMPANIONS
BARE BONES CONFIGURATION GUIDE

CONFIGURING PROCUREMENT AND SOURCING WITHIN DYNAMICS 365 FOR FINANCE & OPERATIONS
MODULE 2: CONFIGURING PROCUREMENT CATEGORIES

Assigning Products To Procurement Categories

How to do it...

Step 8: Update the Product name

This will filter out all of our products to just show the ones with transistor in the name, which are probably all of the products that we want to add to this category.

www.dynamicscompanions.com
Dynamics Companions

- 83 -

www.blindsquirrelpublishing.com
© 2019 Blind Squirrel Publishing, LLC , All Rights Reserved

BLIND SQUIRREL
PUBLISHING

DYNAMICS COMPANIONS
BARE BONES CONFIGURATION GUIDE

CONFIGURING PROCUREMENT AND SOURCING WITHIN DYNAMICS 365 FOR FINANCE & OPERATIONS
MODULE 2: CONFIGURING PROCUREMENT CATEGORIES

Assigning Products To Procurement Categories

How to do it...

Step 9: Selecy 700201 and click ->

We can select products individually and add them to the category.

To do this just select the **700201** record and click on the **->** button.

www.dynamicscompanions.com
Dynamics Companions

- 84 -

www.blindsquirrelpublishing.com
© 2019 Blind Squirrel Publishing, LLC , All Rights Reserved

BLIND SQUIRREL
PUBLISHING

DYNAMICS COMPANIONS
BARE BONES CONFIGURATION GUIDE

CONFIGURING PROCUREMENT AND SOURCING WITHIN DYNAMICS 365 FOR FINANCE & OPERATIONS
MODULE 2: CONFIGURING PROCUREMENT CATEGORIES

Assigning Products To Procurement Categories

How to do it...

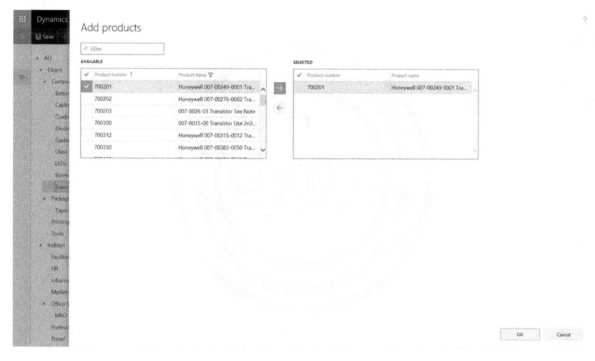

Step 9: Selecy 700201 and click ->

This will add the product to the selected panel on the form and the product is now linked to the hierarchy node.

www.dynamicscompanions.com
Dynamics Companions

- 85 -

www.blindsquirrelpublishing.com
© 2019 Blind Squirrel Publishing, LLC , All Rights Reserved

BLIND SQUIRREL
PUBLISHING

DYNAMICS COMPANIONS
BARE BONES CONFIGURATION GUIDE

CONFIGURING PROCUREMENT AND SOURCING WITHIN DYNAMICS 365 FOR FINANCE & OPERATIONS
MODULE 2: CONFIGURING PROCUREMENT CATEGORIES

Assigning Products To Procurement Categories

How to do it...

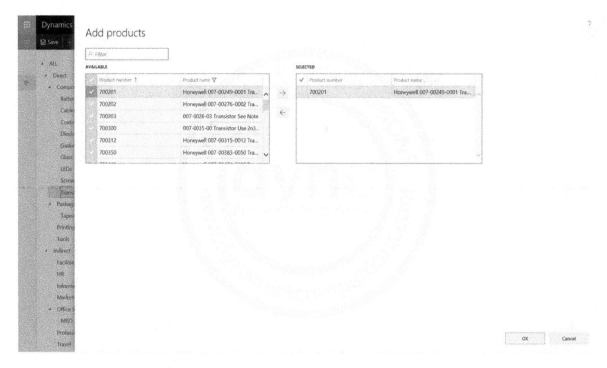

Step 10: Click Select all and click ->

But there is an easier way to do this, and that is to select all of the filtered products and add them to the category.

To do this just click on the **Select all** button and click on the **->** button.

dyn c
www.dynamicscompanions.com
Dynamics Companions

- 86 -

www.blindsquirrelpublishing.com
© 2019 Blind Squirrel Publishing, LLC, All Rights Reserved

BLIND SQUIRREL
PUBLISHING

DYNAMICS COMPANIONS
BARE BONES CONFIGURATION GUIDE

CONFIGURING PROCUREMENT AND SOURCING WITHIN DYNAMICS 365 FOR FINANCE & OPERATIONS
MODULE 2: CONFIGURING PROCUREMENT CATEGORIES

Assigning Products To Procurement Categories

How to do it...

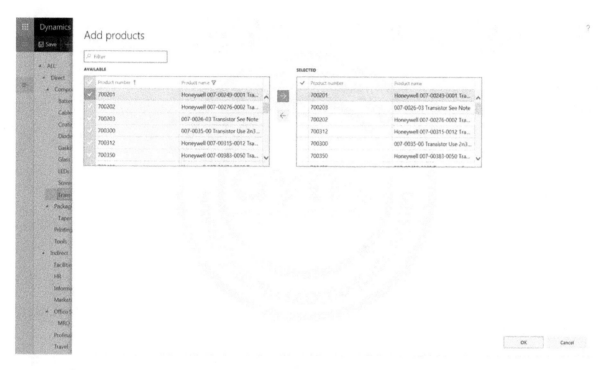

Step 11: Click OK

This will move all of the products over to the selected panel. After we have done that we can exit from the form.

To do this just click on the **OK** button.

dyn c

www.dynamicscompanions.com
Dynamics Companions

- 87 -

www.blindsquirrelpublishing.com
© 2019 Blind Squirrel Publishing, LLC , All Rights Reserved

BLIND SQUIRREL
PUBLISHING

DYNAMICS COMPANIONS
BARE BONES CONFIGURATION GUIDE

CONFIGURING PROCUREMENT AND SOURCING WITHIN DYNAMICS 365 FOR FINANCE & OPERATIONS
MODULE 2: CONFIGURING PROCUREMENT CATEGORIES

Assigning Products To Procurement Categories

How to do it...

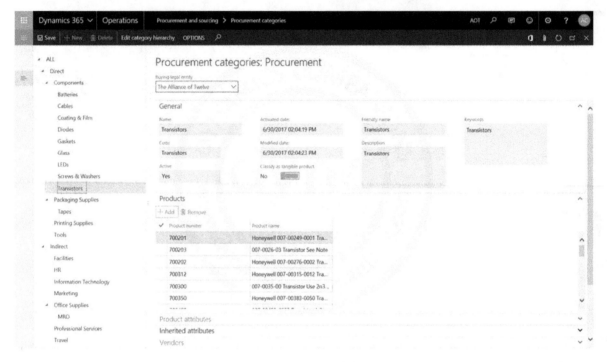

Step 11: Click OK

Now all of the products will show up within the **Products** tab group of the **Procurement Categories**.

dyn c
dynamics companions
www.dynamicscompanions.com
Dynamics Companions

- 88 -

www.blindsquirrelpublishing.com
© 2019 Blind Squirrel Publishing, LLC , All Rights Reserved

BLIND SQUIRREL
PUBLISHING

DYNAMICS COMPANIONS
BARE BONES CONFIGURATION GUIDE

CONFIGURING PROCUREMENT AND SOURCING WITHIN DYNAMICS 365 FOR FINANCE & OPERATIONS
MODULE 2: CONFIGURING PROCUREMENT CATEGORIES

Assigning Products To Procurement Categories

How to do it...

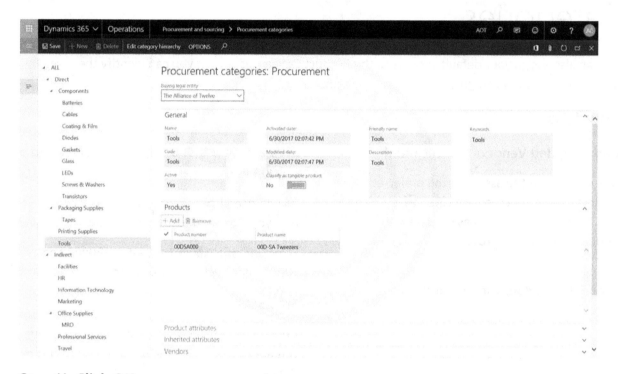

Step 11: Click OK

We can repeat the process for all of the other **Procurement Categories**.

dync
www.dynamicscompanions.com
Dynamics Companions

- 89 -

www.blindsquirrelpublishing.com
© 2019 Blind Squirrel Publishing, LLC , All Rights Reserved

BLIND SQUIRREL
PUBLISHING

DYNAMICS COMPANIONS
BARE BONES CONFIGURATION GUIDE

CONFIGURING PROCUREMENT AND SOURCING WITHIN DYNAMICS 365 FOR FINANCE & OPERATIONS
MODULE 2: CONFIGURING PROCUREMENT CATEGORIES

Assigning Vendors To Procurement Categories

You can also assign your default vendors to the Product Categories so that you can identify the preferred vendors by category.

How to do it...

Step 1: Expand Vendors and click Add

Now we will want to associate the preferred vendors for this procurement categories which we will do in a similar way as we did for the products through the Procurement categories form.

Expand the **Vendors** fast tab and click on the **Add** button.

Step 2: Select 100001, 100002, 100004 and 100008 and click ->

All you need to do is select all of the vendors that you want and assign to the category.

Select vendors **100001, 100002, 100004** and **100008** and click on the **->** button.

Step 3: Click OK

Now our preferred vendors are assigned to our category we can save the updates and return to the categories.

Click on the **OK** button.

DYNAMICS COMPANIONS
BARE BONES CONFIGURATION GUIDE

CONFIGURING PROCUREMENT AND SOURCING WITHIN DYNAMICS 365 FOR FINANCE & OPERATIONS
MODULE 2: CONFIGURING PROCUREMENT CATEGORIES

Assigning Vendors To Procurement Categories

How to do it...

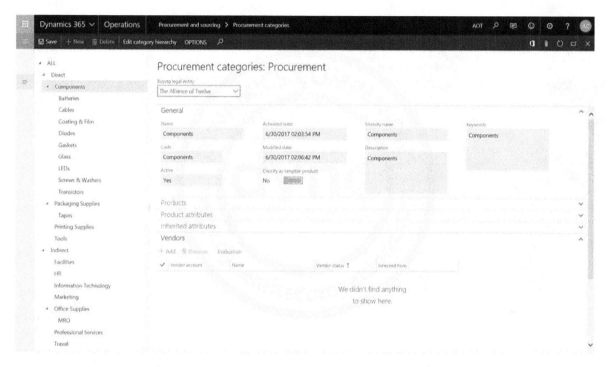

Step 1: Expand Vendors and click Add

Now we will want to associate the preferred vendors for this procurement categories which we will do in a similar way as we did for the products through the Procurement categories form.

To do this just expand the **Vendors** fast tab and click on the **Add** button.

dyn c
www.dynamicscompanions.com
Dynamics Companions

- 91 -

www.blindsquirrelpublishing.com
© 2019 Blind Squirrel Publishing, LLC , All Rights Reserved

BLIND SQUIRREL
PUBLISHING

DYNAMICS COMPANIONS
BARE BONES CONFIGURATION GUIDE

CONFIGURING PROCUREMENT AND SOURCING WITHIN DYNAMICS 365 FOR FINANCE & OPERATIONS
MODULE 2: CONFIGURING PROCUREMENT CATEGORIES

Assigning Vendors To Procurement Categories

How to do it...

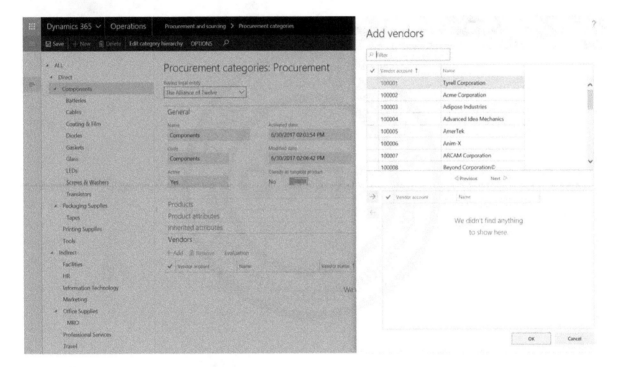

Step 1: Expand Vendors and click Add

This will open up the **Add Vendors** dialog box where we will be able to see the list of vendors that we have configures and the ones that are associated with this category node.

dyn c
dynamics companions

www.dynamicscompanions.com
Dynamics Companions

- 92 -

www.blindsquirrelpublishing.com
© 2019 Blind Squirrel Publishing, LLC , All Rights Reserved

BLIND SQUIRREL
PUBLISHING

DYNAMICS COMPANIONS
BARE BONES CONFIGURATION GUIDE

CONFIGURING PROCUREMENT AND SOURCING WITHIN DYNAMICS 365 FOR FINANCE & OPERATIONS
MODULE 2: CONFIGURING PROCUREMENT CATEGORIES

Assigning Vendors To Procurement Categories

How to do it...

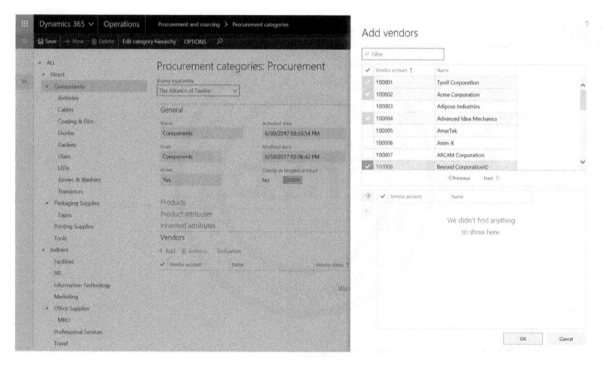

Step 2: Select 100001, 100002, 100004 and 100008 and click ->

All you need to do is select all of the vendors that you want and assign to the category.

To do this just select vendors **100001**, **100002**, **100004** and **100008** and then click on the **->** button.

www.dynamicscompanions.com
Dynamics Companions

- 93 -

www.blindsquirrelpublishing.com
© 2019 Blind Squirrel Publishing, LLC , All Rights Reserved

BLIND SQUIRREL
PUBLISHING

DYNAMICS COMPANIONS
BARE BONES CONFIGURATION GUIDE

CONFIGURING PROCUREMENT AND SOURCING WITHIN DYNAMICS 365 FOR FINANCE & OPERATIONS
MODULE 2: CONFIGURING PROCUREMENT CATEGORIES

Assigning Vendors To Procurement Categories

How to do it...

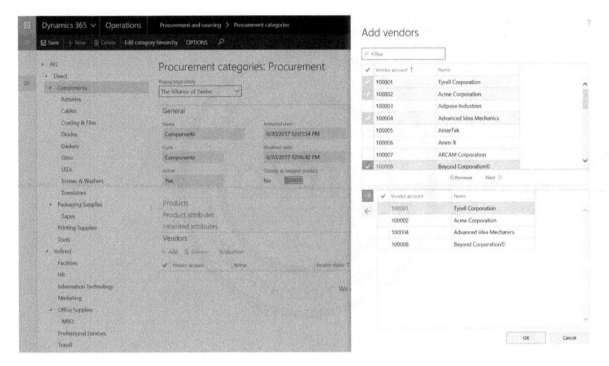

Step 3: Click OK

Now our preferred vendors are assigned to our category we can save the updates and return to the categories.

To do this just click on the **OK** button.

dync
www.dynamicscompanions.com
Dynamics Companions

- 94 -

www.blindsquirrelpublishing.com
© 2019 Blind Squirrel Publishing, LLC , All Rights Reserved

BLIND SQUIRREL
PUBLISHING

DYNAMICS COMPANIONS
BARE BONES CONFIGURATION GUIDE

CONFIGURING PROCUREMENT AND SOURCING WITHIN DYNAMICS 365 FOR FINANCE & OPERATIONS
MODULE 2: CONFIGURING PROCUREMENT CATEGORIES

Assigning Vendors To Procurement Categories

How to do it...

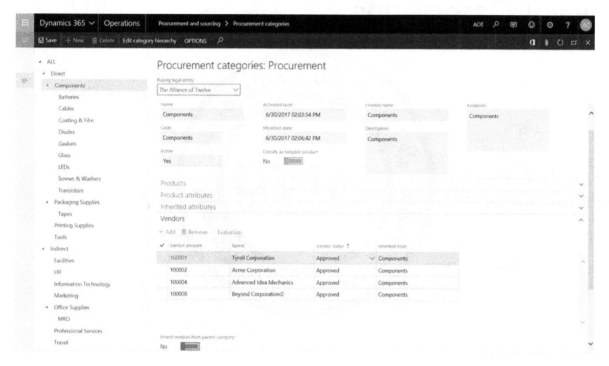

Step 3: Click OK

When we return back to the **Procurement Categories** form we will see that the vendors have been added to the category.

We can keep on updating all of the other categories if we like.

dyn c
www.dynamicscompanions.com
Dynamics Companions

- 95 -

www.blindsquirrelpublishing.com
© 2019 Blind Squirrel Publishing, LLC , All Rights Reserved

BLIND SQUIRREL
PUBLISHING

DYNAMICS COMPANIONS
BARE BONES CONFIGURATION GUIDE

CONFIGURING PROCUREMENT AND SOURCING WITHIN DYNAMICS 365 FOR FINANCE & OPERATIONS
MODULE 2: CONFIGURING PROCUREMENT CATEGORIES

Inheriting Approved Vendors From Parent Categories

There is a nifty feature within the Categories maintenance form for both the products and vendors which allows child categories to inherit values form their parent categories. This can save a lot of rekeying if you take advantage of it.

How to do it...

Step 1: Select Transistors

Now we will want to select the child node that we want to inherit all of the properties from the parent category node from.

Select the **Transistors** node.

Step 2: Toggle the Inherit vendors from parent category

All you need to do is mark the record to **Inherit Vendors from Parent Category** flag and the parents vendors will automatically populate from the parent.

Toggle the Inherit vendors from parent category switch and set it to Yes.

DYNAMICS COMPANIONS
BARE BONES CONFIGURATION GUIDE

CONFIGURING PROCUREMENT AND SOURCING WITHIN DYNAMICS 365 FOR FINANCE & OPERATIONS
MODULE 2: CONFIGURING PROCUREMENT CATEGORIES

Inheriting Approved Vendors From Parent Categories

How to do it...

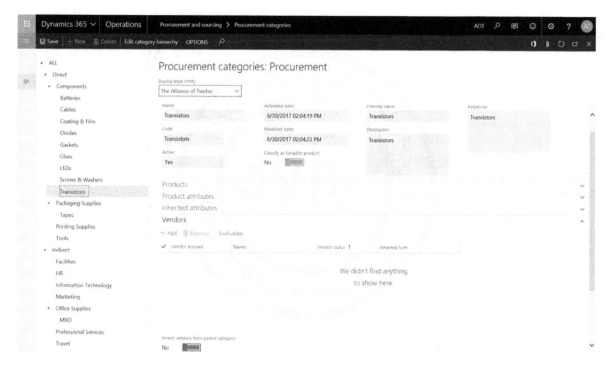

Step 1: Select Transistors

Now we will want to select the child node that we want to inherit all of the properties from the parent category node from.

To do this just select the **Transistors** node.

www.dynamicscompanions.com
Dynamics Companions

- 97 -

www.blindsquirrelpublishing.com
© 2019 Blind Squirrel Publishing, LLC , All Rights Reserved

BLIND SQUIRREL
PUBLISHING

DYNAMICS COMPANIONS
BARE BONES CONFIGURATION GUIDE

CONFIGURING PROCUREMENT AND SOURCING WITHIN DYNAMICS 365 FOR FINANCE & OPERATIONS
MODULE 2: CONFIGURING PROCUREMENT CATEGORIES

Inheriting Approved Vendors From Parent Categories

How to do it...

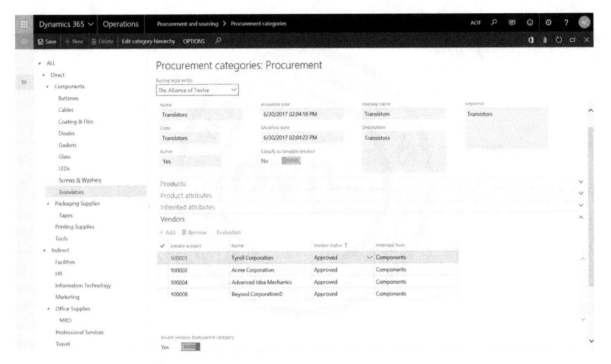

Step 2: Toggle the Inherit vendors from parent category

All you need to do is mark the record to **Inherit Vendors from Parent Category** flag and the parents vendors will automatically populate from the parent.

To do this we will just need to toggle the **Inherit vendors from parent category** option.

For this example, we will want to click on the **Inherit vendors from parent category** toggle switch and set it to the **Yes** value.

We will see that now all of the preferred vendors that we set up in the parent node have been automatically inherited.

dync
dynamics companions

www.dynamicscompanions.com
Dynamics Companions

- 98 -

www.blindsquirrelpublishing.com
© 2019 Blind Squirrel Publishing, LLC , All Rights Reserved

BLIND SQUIRREL
PUBLISHING

DYNAMICS COMPANIONS
BARE BONES CONFIGURATION GUIDE

CONFIGURING PROCUREMENT AND SOURCING WITHIN DYNAMICS 365 FOR FINANCE & OPERATIONS
MODULE 2: CONFIGURING PROCUREMENT CATEGORIES

Inheriting Approved Vendors From Parent Categories

Summary

How cool is that. We have now categorized our products into procurement categories and also set up preferred vendors.

www.dynamicscompanions.com
Dynamics Companions

- 99 -

www.blindsquirrelpublishing.com
© 2019 Blind Squirrel Publishing, LLC, All Rights Reserved

BLIND SQUIRREL
PUBLISHING

DYNAMICS COMPANIONS
BARE BONES CONFIGURATION GUIDE

CONFIGURING PROCUREMENT AND SOURCING WITHIN DYNAMICS 365 FOR FINANCE & OPERATIONS
MODULE 2: CONFIGURING PROCUREMENT CATEGORIES

Review

Congratulations. You have now started to organize your products by creating procurement categories and linked them to your products and vendors. Now you can start working on alphabetizing your spice rack.

www.dynamicscompanions.com
Dynamics Companions

- 100 -

www.blindsquirrelpublishing.com
© 2019 Blind Squirrel Publishing, LLC , All Rights Reserved

BLIND SQUIRREL
PUBLISHING

DYNAMICS COMPANIONS
BARE BONES CONFIGURATION GUIDE

CONFIGURING PROCUREMENT AND SOURCING WITHIN DYNAMICS 365 FOR FINANCE & OPERATIONS
MODULE 2: CONFIGURING PROCUREMENT CATEGORIES

About The Author

Murray Fife is an Author of over 20 books on Microsoft Dynamics including the Bare Bones Configuration Guide series. These guides comprise of over 15 books which step you through the setup and configuration of Microsoft Dynamics including Finance, Operations, Human Resources, Production, Service Management, and Project Accounting.

Throughout his 25+ years of experience in the software industry he has worked in many different roles during his career, including as a developer, an implementation consultant, a trainer and a demo guy within the partner channel which gives him a great understanding of the requirements for both customers and partners perspective.

If you are interested in contacting Murray or want to follow his blogs and posts then here is all of his contact information:

Email: murray@murrayfife.com

Twitter: @murrayfife
Facebook: facebook.com/murraycfife
Google: google.com/+murrayfife
LinkedIn: linkedin.com/in/murrayfife

Blog: atinkerersnotebook.com
Slideshare: slideshare.net/murrayfife
Amazon: amazon.com/author/murrayfife

dync
www.dynamicscompanions.com
Dynamics Companions

- 101 -

www.blindsquirrelpublishing.com
© 2019 Blind Squirrel Publishing, LLC , All Rights Reserved

BLIND SQUIRREL
PUBLISHING

DYNAMICS COMPANIONS
BARE BONES CONFIGURATION GUIDE

CONFIGURING PROCUREMENT AND SOURCING WITHIN DYNAMICS 365 FOR FINANCE & OPERATIONS
MODULE 2: CONFIGURING PROCUREMENT CATEGORIES

Need More Help with Microsoft Dynamics AX 2012 or Dynamics 365 for Operations

We are firm believers that Microsoft Dynamics AX 2012 or Dynamics 365 is not a hard product to learn, but the problem is where do you start. Which is why we developed the Bare Bones Configuration Guides. The aim of this series is to step you though the configuration of Microsoft Dynamics from a blank system, and then step you through the setup of all of the core modules within Microsoft Dynamics. We start with the setup of a base system, then move on to the financial, distribution, and operations modules.

Each book builds upon the previous ones, and by the time you have worked through all of the guides then you will have completely configured a simple (but functional) Microsoft Dynamics instance. To make it even more worthwhile you will have a far better understanding of Microsoft Dynamics and also how everything fits together.

As of now there are 16 guides in this series broken out as follows:

- Configuring a Training Environment
- Configuring an Organization
- Configuring the General Ledger
- Configuring Cash and Bank Management
- Configuring Accounts Receivable
- Configuring Accounts Payable
- Configuring Product Information Management
- Configuring Inventory Management

- Configuring Procurement and Sourcing
- Configuring Sales Order Management
- Configuring Human Resource Management
- Configuring Project Management and Accounting
- Configuring Production Control
- Configuring Sales and Marketing
- Configuring Service Management
- Configuring Warehouse Management

Although you can get each of these guides individually, and we think that each one is a great Visual resources to step you through each of the particular modules, for those of you that want to take full advantage of the series, you will want to start from the beginning and work through them one by one. After you have done that you would have done people told me was impossible for one persons to do, and that is to configure all of the core modules within Microsoft Dynamics.

If you are interested in finding out more about the series and also view all of the details including topics covered within the module, then browse to the Bare Bones Configuration Guide landing page on the Microsoft Dynamics Companions website. You will find all of the details, and also downloadable resources that help you with the setup of Microsoft Dynamics. Here is the full link: http://www.dynamicscompanions.com/

dyn c
www.dynamicscompanions.com
Dynamics Companions

- 103 -

www.blindsquirrelpublishing.com
© 2019 Blind Squirrel Publishing, LLC , All Rights Reserved

BLIND SQUIRREL
PUBLISHING